I0660589

Just
the
Facts

A POCKET GUIDE TO BASIC NURSING

Just the Facts

A POCKET GUIDE TO BASIC NURSING

Third Edition

Veronica "Ronnie" Peterson
BA, RN, BSN, MS

Clinical Staff Educator,
University of Wisconsin Medical Foundation;

Adjunct Clinical Instructor,
University of Wisconsin School of Nursing,
Madison, Wisconsin

with 93 illustrations

Mosby

An Affiliate of Elsevier Science

An Affiliate of Elsevier Science

11830 Westline Industrial Drive
St. Louis, Missouri 63146

Third Edition

NOTICE

Nursing is an ever-changing field. Standard safety precautions must be followed, but as new research and clinical experience broaden our knowledge, changes in treatment and drug therapy may become necessary or appropriate. Readers are advised to check the most current product information provided by the manufacturer of each drug to be administered to verify the recommended dose, the method and duration of administration, and contraindications. It is the responsibility of the licensed prescriber, relying on experience and knowledge of the patient, to determine dosages and the best treatment for each individual patient. Neither the publisher nor the author assumes any liability for any injury and/or damage to persons or property arising from this publication.

Vice President and Publishing Director: Sally Schrefer
Executive Editor: Susan R. Epstein
Developmental Editor: Linda Stagg
Publication Services Manager: John Rogers
Project Manager: Mary Turner
Senior Designer: Kathi Gosche
Cover Design: Renée Duenow

Printed in the United States of America

ISBN 9997640225

03 04 05 06 CL/RRD-C 9 8 7 6 5 4 3

Reviewers

Roberta Goeckner, PharmD
Clinical Pharmacist,
Gateway Regional Medical Center,
Granite City, Illinois

Claudia Louth Mitchell, RN, BSN, MSN
Professor of Nursing,
Santa Barbara City College,
Santa Barbara, California

Cheryl M. Prandoni, RN, BSN, MSN
Director of Learning Resources, School of Nursing,
The Catholic University of America,
Washington, DC

Student Reviewers:
Renee Green, RN Student
Fayetteville, North Carolina

Mary Jo Matzke, PA Student
Chicago, Illinois

Nicole Miller, PA Student
Mobile, Alabama

Kjerstine Siebert, LPN Student
Madison, Wisconsin

Preface

When I began my first student clinical experience, I felt overwhelmed. There just wasn't time to memorize lab values, metric conversions, or the dozens of other facts I needed to know. So I compiled a small notebook of this information and carried it with me everywhere. Later, as a graduate student pursuing my master's degree, I taught nursing students who were experiencing the same problem.

For them, and for you, I have compiled those hard-to-memorize charts, graphs, numbers, and abbreviations that you must know, even in your first clinical experience. I've added some handy checklists for physical assessment and an assortment of other useful bits of information.

Just the Facts: A Pocket Guide to Basic Nursing is designed to be a portable, quick reference for facts and figures, focusing on adult health care. I hope you will find this as handy a resource during your clinical work as I did.

Ronnie Peterson

Contents

Just
the
Facts

**A POCKET GUIDE
TO BASIC NURSING**

Chapter 1

Health Care Terminology

For an in-depth study of health care terminology, consult the following publications:

Anderson KN, Anderson LE, Glanze WD: *Mosby's medical, nursing, & allied health dictionary,* ed 5, St Louis, 1998, Mosby.

Austrin MG, Austrin HR: *Learning medical terminology,* ed 9, St Louis, 1998, Mosby.

Birmingham JJ: *Medical terminology: a self-learning text,* ed 3, St Louis, 1999, Mosby.

Brooker CG: *Mosby's nurse's pocket dictionary,* ed 32, St Louis, 2002, Mosby.

Thibodeau G, Patton K: *Structure and function of the human body,* ed 11, St Louis, 2000, Mosby.

ABBREVIATIONS*

a before
aa of each
AA Alcoholics Anonymous; ascending aorta
AAA abdominal aortic aneurysm
abd abdomen; abdominal
ABG arterial blood gas
abn abnormal
abp arterial blood pressure
ac before meals
ACTH adrenocorticotropic hormone
ad lib as desired
ADH antidiuretic hormone
ADLs activities of daily living
AIDS acquired immunodeficiency syndrome
AK above the knee
AKA above the knee amputation
ALL acute lymphocytic leukemia
ALS amyotrophic lateral sclerosis
am morning
ama against medical advice
amb ambulatory
AML acute monocytic (myelogenous) leukemia
amp ampicillin; amputation
amt amount
ANS autonomic nervous system
A&O alert and oriented
AODA alcohol and other drug abuse
A&P auscultation and percussion
appy appendectomy
Aq water
ARC AIDS-related complex; American Red Cross
ARDS adult respiratory distress syndrome
as left ear
ASA aspirin

---

*Standard abbreviations may vary by institution.

ASAP as soon as possible
ASL American Sign Language
AU both ears
AV atrioventricular
AVR aortic valve replacement
A&W alive and well

Ba barium
BAC blood alcohol concentration
BB breakthrough bleeding
BBB blood-brain barrier; bundle-branch block
BBT basal body temperature
BE barium enema
bid twice per day
BK below the knee
BKA below the knee amputation
BL bleeding; baseline; blood loss
BLE both lower extremities
BM bowel movement; body mass; bone marrow
BMR basal metabolic rate
bolus medication given IV in a short period of time
BP blood pressure; bathroom privileges; birth place
BPH benign prostatic hypertrophy
BRBPR bright red blood per rectum
BR bed rest
BRP bathroom privileges
BS blood sugar; bowel sounds; breath sounds
BSA body surface area
BT bleeding time; brain tumor; bladder tumor
BUE both upper extremities
BUN blood urea nitrogen
BV blood volume
BW body weight; birth weight
Bx biopsy

c̄ with
C Celsius; calorie; Caucasian
CA cancer

C&A Clinitest and Acetest
CABG coronary artery bypass graft
CAD coronary artery disease
CAT computerized axial tomography
cath catheter; catheterization
CBC complete blood count
CBI continuous bladder irrigation
cbr complete bed rest
CBS chronic brain syndrome
cc cubic centimeter
CC chief complaint
CCU coronary care unit
CD cadaver donor; cardiac disease
CDC Centers for Disease Control and Prevention
CEA carotid endarterectomy
CF cystic fibrosis; cardiac failure
cg centigram
CHD coronary heart disease; congenital heart disease
CHF congestive heart failure
CHO carbohydrate
CIS carcinoma in situ
cl clear liquid diet
Cl chlorine
CLD chronic liver (lung) disease
cm centimeter; costal margin
cm³ cubic centimeter
CMV cytomegalovirus
CNS central nervous system
c/o complains of
CO carbon monoxide; cardiac output; castor oil
CO₂ carbon dioxide
comp complaint; complication; compound
COPD chronic obstructive pulmonary disease
CP cerebral palsy; closing pressure
CPK creatine phosphokinase
CRD chronic renal disease
CRF chronic renal failure

crit hematocrit
c-sec cesarean section
CS central supply/central service; coronary sinus
C&S culture and sensitivity
CSF cerebrospinal fluid; colony-stimulating factor
CST convulsive shock therapy
CSW certified social worker
CT computed tomography
CV cell volume; central venous
CVA cerebral vascular attack
CVP central venous pressure
CVS cardiovascular system
CXR chest x-ray
cysto cystoscopy

d day
DAT diet as tolerated
dc discontinue
D&C dilatation and curettage
D/C discharge
DDS Doctor of Dental Surgery
DG diagnosis; diastolic gallop
DIC disseminated intravascular coagulation
diff differential blood count
DJD degenerative joint disease
DM diabetes mellitus; diastolic murmur
DNR do not resuscitate
DOA dead on arrival
DOB date of birth
DOD date of death
DOE dyspneic on exertion
DPT diphtheria/pertussis/tetanus
DTR deep tendon reflex
DU duodenal ulcer
DVT deep vein thrombosis
DW distilled water; dry weight
D5W 5% dextrose in water
dx diagnosis; dextran

EA each
EBL estimated blood loss
EBV Epstein-Barr virus
ECF extracellular fluid
ECG electrocardiogram
ECT electroconvulsive therapy
ED effective dose; emergency department
EDD estimated date of delivery
EEG electroencephalogram
(E)ENT (eye) ear, nose, throat
EKG electrocardiogram
EL elixir
EMG electromyogram
EN enema
eom extraocular movement
EP ectopic pregnancies
ER emergency department; ejection rate
ESP extrasensory perception
ESRD end-stage renal disease
EST electroshock therapy
ET endotracheal; etiology; effective temperature
ETOH alcohol

F Fahrenheit; father; female
FBP femoral blood pressure
FBS fasting blood sugar
f/c/s fever, chills, sweats
FD fatal dose; forceps delivery
FEV forced expiratory volume
FF force fluids; fat free; flat feet; foster father
FFP fresh-frozen plasma
FHR fetal heart rate
fl fluid or full liquid diet
FOB foot of the bed
FP false positive; family practice; frozen plasma
FSH follicle-stimulating hormone
FUO fever of unknown origin
FV fluid volume

fx fracture; family
Fx Hx family history

g gram
GB gallbladder; Guillain-Barré syndrome
GC gonococcus
GH growth hormone
GI gastrointestinal
gm gram
GP general practitioner
gr grain
grav I, II, III, etc. pregnancy one, two, three, etc.
GT gastrostomy tube
GTH gonadotropic hormone
gtt drops
GTT glucose tolerance test
GU genitourinary
GYN gynecology

h hour; height; high; hormone
HA headache; high anxiety
HAV hepatitis A virus
Hb hemoglobin
HB heart block; hemoglobin; house bound
HBV hepatitis B virus
hCG human chorionic gonadotropin
Hct hematocrit
HD heart disease; Hodgkin's disease
HGH human growth hormone
H&H hemoglobin and hematocrit
HIV human immunodeficiency virus (AIDS)
HL hearing loss
HLA human lymphocyte antigen
HO house officer; high oxygen
HOB head of the bed
hr hour
HR heart rate; hospital record
hs at bedtime

HS herpes simplex; house surgeon
HSV herpes simplex virus
HTN hypertension
HVD hypertensive vascular disease
hx history
hypo hypodermic

IC inspiratory capacity; intercostal; intracellular; intracerebral; intracranial
ICP intracranial pressure
ICS intercostal space
ICU intensive care unit
ID infant death; ineffective dose; intradermal
I&D incision and drainage
IDDM insulin-dependent diabetes mellitus
IE immunoelectrophoresis
Ig immunoglobulin
IH infectious hepatitis
IM intramuscular; infectious mononucleosis
IN intranasal
I&O intake and output
IOP intraocular pressure
IP intraperitoneal; interphalangeal
IPPB intermittent positive pressure breathing
irr irregular
IS in situ; intercostal space; interspace
IT inhalation test; intratracheal tube
ITT insulin tolerance test
IUD intrauterine device
IV intravenous; intravascular
IVP intravenous push
IVPB IV piggyback

JEJ jejunum
JRA juvenile rheumatoid arthritis
JV jugular vein (venous)
JVD jugular vein distention
JVP jugular vein pressure (pulse)

K absolute zero; Kelvin
K$^+$ potassium
kg kilogram
KJ knee jerk
KUB kidney/ureter/bladder
KVO keep vein open

L liter; left; length; low; lower
LA lactic acid; left arm; left atrial; left atrium
LAD left anterior descending (coronary artery)
LAP left atrial pressure
lat lateral
LBBB left bundle-branch block
LCA left coronary artery
LCH left costal margin
LD lethal dose; left deltoid; living donor
LE lower extremity; left eye
LFD lactose-free diet; least fatal dose
LFT liver function tests
LGH lactogenic hormone
LH luteinizing hormone
LL left leg; left lower; left lung
LLE left lower extremity
LLL left lower lobe
LLQ left lower quadrant
LMP last menstrual period
LOA leave of absence
LOC loss of consciousness
LOM loss of motion
LP lumbar puncture; low protein
LPN licensed practical nurse
LS lumbar sacral; left side; liver and spleen
LSB left sternal border
LT left; left thigh; long term
LUE left upper extremity
LUL left upper lobe
LUQ left upper quadrant
LV left ventricle; live vaccine
LVH left ventricular hypertrophy

m meter; minim
M murmur; male; married; minute; month; mother
MA mental age
MAP mean arterial pressure
MD medical doctor; manic depressive; medium dose; muscular dystrophy
ME medical examiner; middle ear
MED minimal effective dose
mEq milliequivalent
mg milligram
Mg magnesium
MG myasthenia gravis
MI myocardial infarction; mitral insufficiency
ml milliliter
ML middle lobe; midline
mm millimeter
MM mucous membrane; malignant melanoma; multiple myeloma
mm³ cubic millimeter
mm Hg millimeters of mercury
MP mean pressure; menstrual period
MR mental retardation; metabolic rate; mitral reflux
MRI magnetic resonance imaging
MRSA methicillin-resistant *Staphylococcus aureus*
MS multiple sclerosis; mitral stenosis
MSL midsternal line
MSO₄ morphine sulfate
MSW master's degree in social work
MV mitral valve

N nasal; nerve; normal
Na sodium
NAD no appreciable disease
NAS no added salt
NC no casualty; not cultured
ND no disease; normal delivery
NE no effect; not evaluated

NF normal flow; not found
ng nasogastric
NH nursing home
NI no information; not identified
NIDDM non–insulin-dependent diabetes mellitus
NIH National Institutes of Health (Bethesda, Md.)
NKDA no known drug allergies
noc night
NPN nonprotein nitrogen
NPO nothing by mouth
NR do not repeat; no response; not readable
NS normal saline; nervous system; no sample; not sufficient
NT nasotracheal; not tested
N&V nausea and vomiting

O eye; none; opening; oral
OB obstetrics
OBS organic brain syndrome
OC office call; on call; oral contraceptive
OD overdose; right eye
OH occupational history
OL left eye
OM otitis media
OOB out of bed
OP opening pressure; osmotic pressure
OR operating room
ORIF open reduction internal fixation
OS left eye; mouth; oral surgery
OT occupational therapy
OTC over the counter
OU both eyes

p after; position; pressure; protein; pulse; pupil
PA physician's assistant; pathology; primary anemia; pulmonary artery
P&A posterior/anterior
Paco$_2$ partial pressure of carbon dioxide (arterial)

Pao$_2$ partial pressure of oxygen (arterial)
Pap Papanicolaou test (smear)
PAR postanesthesia room
pat paroxysmal atrial tachycardia
pc after meals; platelet count; pulmonic closure
PCA patient-controlled analgesia
PCN penicillin
Pco$_2$ partial pressure of carbon dioxide
PCV packed cell volume
PCWP pulmonary capillary wedge pressure
PD postural drainage; papilla diameter; poorly differentiated
PDR *Physicians' Desk Reference*
PE physical examination; pleural effusion; pulmonary emboli
PEEP positive end-expiratory pressure
PEG pneumoencephalogram
PERRLA pupils equal, round, reactive to light, and accommodating
PET positron emission tomography
PG pregnant; prostaglandin
pH hydrogen ion concentration
PI present illness; pulmonary infarction
PID pelvic inflammatory disease
PKU phenylketonuria
pm afternoon
PM post mortem
PMH past medical history
PMS premenstrual syndrome
PN percussion note; pneumonia
PO by mouth; postop
Po$_2$ partial pressure of oxygen
poly many
PP partial pressure; pink puffers (emphysema)
PR per rectum; practical remission; peripheral resistance; pulse rate
PRN as needed
PS per second; physical status; *Pseudomonas*

pt patient; pint
PT physical therapy; parathyroid; pneumothorax
PTT partial thromboplastin time
PUD peptic ulcer disease
PV peripheral vascular; peripheral vein
PVC premature ventricular contraction; pulmonary
    venous congestion
PVD peripheral vascular disease
PUR post void residual

q every; quart
qd every day
qh every hour
q2h, q3h, etc. every 2 hours, every 3 hours, etc.
qhs every evening
qid four times a day
ql as much as desired
qn every night
qns quantity not sufficient
QOD every other day
QPM every night
qs quantity sufficient
QT quiet
QV as much as you like

R right; radiology; rectal; remote; resistance
RA rheumatoid arthritis; renal artery; right arm;
    right atrium
rad radiation unit; radical; right axis deviation
RAP right atrial pressure
RAS renal artery stenosis
RBBB right bundle-branch block
RBC red blood cell
RCA right coronary artery
RCM right costal margin; red cell mass
RDA recommended daily allowance; right
    dorsoanterior
RE right eye

REM rapid eye movement
rep repeat
RF rheumatic fever; releasing factor
Rh rhesus factor
RHD rheumatic heart disease
RL right leg (lung)
RLE right lower extremity
RLL right lower lobe
RLQ right lower quadrant
RM radical mastectomy; respiratory movement
RML right middle lobe
RN registered nurse
R/O rule out
ROM range of motion
ROS review of systems
RP refractory period; resting pressure
RPA right pulmonary artery
RR respiratory rate
RRR regular rate and rhythm
RT respiratory therapy; radiation therapy; reaction time
RUA routine urinalysis
RUE right upper extremity
RUL right upper lobe
RUQ right upper quadrant
RV residual volume; respiratory volume
Rx treatment or medications

s without; sacral; salmonella; single; smooth
SA salicylic acid; sarcoma; surface area
SB sternal border; single breath; stillbirth
SBO small bowel obstruction
SC subcutaneous; semiclosed; sickle cell; sugar coated
SD skin dose; septal defect; standard; standard deviation; sudden death
SF scarlet fever; spinal fluid
SG skin graft; specific gravity

SH serum hepatitis; sex hormone
SI sacroiliac; serum iron
SIDS sudden infant death syndrome
sig let it be labeled
SL under the tongue
SLE systemic lupus erythematosus
SM simple mastectomy; systolic murmur
SN suprasternal notch
SO salpingo-oophorectomy
SOB short of breath; shortness of breath
SOBOE short of breath on exertion
SOS if necessary
S/P status post
sp gr specific gravity
SQ subcutaneous; social quotient; square
sr sedimentation rate; sinus rhythm
ss a half; side to side
ST let it stand; straight; subtotal
STAT immediately
STD sexually transmitted disease
STS serologic test for syphilis
SUD sudden unexplained death
SV severe; stroke volume
SVT supraventricular tachycardia
sx symptom; signs
sz schizophrenia

t teaspoon
T temperature; time; temporal; tumor; tablespoon
T$_3$ triiodothyronine
T$_4$ tetraiodothyronine
T&A tonsillectomy and adenoidectomy
TAH total abdominal hysterectomy
TB tuberculosis; total base; total body
TBG thyroxin-binding globulin
TBI total body irradiation
tbsp tablespoon
TBW total body water (weight)

T&C type and crossmatch
TCDB turn, cough, and deep breathe
TD therapy (treatment) discontinued
TE tetanus; tooth extracted
tea teaspoon
TF total flow; tubular fluid
TG triglycerides
TIA transient ischemic attack
TIBC total iron-binding capacity
tid three times a day
TKO to keep open
TL time lapse; time limited; total lipids
TLC total lung capacity
TM tympanic membrane
TN total negatives; true negative
TNM tumor, nodes, metastasis
TPN total parenteral nutrition
TPR temperature/pulse/respiration
TS test solution; total solids; triple strength
TSA tumor-specific antigen
TSH thyroid-stimulating hormone
TSI triple-sugar iron
tsp teaspoon
TSP total serum protein
TST triple-sugar iron test
TT thrombin time; total thyroxine
TURP transurethral resection of the prostate
tus cough
TV tidal volume; trial visit
TVC total volume capacity
twe tap water enema
Tx treatment

U unit; unknown; upper; urology
UA urinalysis; uric acid
UA/UC urinalysis with cultures
UD urethral discharge
UE upper extremity

UK unknown; urokinase
U/O urine output
URI upper respiratory infection
USP United States Pharmacopeia
ut dict as directed
UTI urinary tract infection
UV ultraviolet; urinary volume

V vein; vision; voice; volume
VA visual acuity
VB viable birth
VC vital capacity; vena cava
VD venereal disease; vapor density
VDH valvular disease/heart
VDRL Venereal Disease Research Laboratory (test for syphilis)
VF field of vision; ventricular fibrillation
VH vaginal hysterectomy; viral hepatitis
VO verbal order
VP vasopressin; venipuncture; venous pressure
VR vocal resonance; right arm; valve replacement; venous return
VRE vancomycin-resistant *Enterococcus*
VS vital signs; verbal scale
VSD ventricular septal defect
VT tidal volume; ventricular tachycardia
VW vessel wall
VZ varicella-zoster

w watt; water; week; weight; wife
WB weight bearing; whole blood
WBC white blood cell; white blood cell count
w/c wheelchair
WC ward clerk; white blood cell; whooping cough
WD well developed; well differentiated
WL waiting list; workload
WM white male; whole milk
WNL within normal limits

WR Wassermann reactions
WT weight; white
W/V weight/volume

Y year
yd yard
YF yellow fever
YO year(s) old
yr year
ys yellow spot (retina)

PREFIXES

a, an absent
ab away from
ad to or toward
aer air
angio blood vessel
ante before
arteri artery
aud ear

bi two
brady slow

cardi heart
cephal head
cerebro brain
chole gallbladder
chondr cartilage
cirrho yellow
co, con with, together
colo colon
contra opposing
cost rib
cran head
crani skull
cyano blue
cysto liquid-filled
    urinary bladder

dactyl fingers/toes
de down, from
dent (o) teeth
derma skin
dis away, separate
dys bad, difficult

e without
encephala brain
endo within, inside
enter intestines
epi on, over
erythro red
ex, extra outside of

gastr stomach
glyco sugar

hem blood
hemato blood
hemi one half
hepat liver
hyper above, beyond
hypo beneath, below

ileo ileum
ili ilium
inter between
intra/intro within

leuko white
lingu tongue
lip fat
litho stone

macro large
mal bad
mega large
melano black
mesi, meso middle
meta change

micro small
mono one
multi many
my muscle
myel bone marrow
myelo spinal cord

neo new, recent
nephr kidney
neuro nervous system

ophthalm eye
osteo bone
ot ear

par near
para beside, near
per through
peri around
phag eat
phleg vein
pneum lung
polio gray
poly many
post after

pre/pro before
proct rectal
psycho the mind

re back
ren kidney
retro back
rhin nose
rhino nose

semi half
splen spleen
spondyl spinal cord
sub below
super above
supra above

tachy fast
tetra four
tri three

uni one

vascular blood vessel
venous vein

Body Fluids

aqua water
chol(e) bile
dacry(o) tears
galact(o) milk
hem(a) blood
hemat(o) blood
hydro water
lacrima tears
mucus secretions from membranes
plasma blood
ptyal(o) saliva
pus liquid inflammation
sangui blood
sanguin(o) very bloody
serum clear portion of blood
urea, uro urine

Body Substances and Chemicals

adip(o) fat
amyl(o) starch
cerumen earwax
collagen connective tissue
ele(o), ole(o) oil
ferrum iron
glyc(o) sugar
hal(o) salt
hyal(o) translucent
lapis stone
lip(o), lipid fat, fatty
lith(o) stone or calculus
mel(i) honey, sugar
natrium sodium
petrous stony hardness
sabum sebaceous gland
sacchar(o) sugar
sal salt

Colors

albus white
chlor(o) green
chrom(o) color
cirrhos orange, yellow
cyan(o) blue
erythr(o) red
leuc(o) white
lutein yellow
melan(o) black
poli(o) gray
rhod(o) red
ruber red
rubor red
xanth(o) yellow

SUFFIXES

ac, al pertaining to
algia pain
ate, ize use, subject

cele protrusion
centesis puncture to remove fluid
cle, cule small
cyte cell

dynia pain

ectomy removal
emesis vomit
emia blood
ent, er, ist person
esis, tion condition

genic origin
gram/graphy written record
graph instrument that records

ia, ism, ity condition
iasis presence of
ible, ile capable
itis inflammation

logy study of

megaly enlargement

ola, ole small
oma tumor

osis, sis abnormal
ostomy opening
ous, tic pertaining to
oxia oxygen

pathy disease
penia deficiency of
pexy, pexis fixation
phagia, phagy eating
phobia fear
plasty surgical shaping
pnea breathing
ptosis prolapse, down

rrhage excessive flow
rrhage, rrhagia suturing
rrhea flow
rrhexis suture

scope examination instrument
scopy examination
stomy surgical opening

tic relating to
tion condition
tome instrument
tomy incision

ule small
ulum small
ulus small
uria urine

SYMBOLS

♀	standing	≤	less than or equal to
♀	sitting	>	greater than
⟳	lying	≥	greater than or equal to
↑	increasing	≈	about
↓	decreasing	ø	none or no
R	right	→	leading to
L	left	@	at
♀	female	♀♀♀♀♀♀	one, two, three
♂	male	#	number
ℨ	dram	"	seconds
℥	ounce	μg	microgram
°	degree	μm	micrometer
′	minute	❏	male
° C	Celsius	○	female
° F	Fahrenheit	+	not definite
®	registered trademark	∨	systolic blood pressure
*	birth	∧	diastolic blood pressure
⊤	death		
⊖	normal		
×	times		
=	equal to		
<	less than		

MEDICAL SPECIALISTS

Allergist Treats the body's reactions to unusual sensitivity

Anesthesiologist Provides anesthesia

Cardiac surgeon Surgically treats conditions and diseases of the heart and chest cavity vessels

Cardiologist Treats conditions and diseases of the heart and blood vessels

Dermatologist Treats conditions and diseases of the skin

Endocrinologist Treats conditions and diseases of the endocrine system

Family practitioner Treats clients of all ages with medical methods

Gastroenterologist Treats conditions and diseases of the digestive tract

General practitioner Treats clients of all ages with medical methods

Geneticist Specialist in the study of genetics

Gerontologist Treats conditions and diseases related to the elderly

Gynecologist Treats conditions and diseases of the female reproductive system

Hematologist Treats blood disorders

Intensivist Monitors and treats people in the intensive care unit

Internist Treats nonsurgical conditions and diseases in adults and children

Medical examiner Performs autopsies, analyzes autopsy and pathology evidence related to a crime

Neonatologist Treats conditions and diseases in newborns, particularly premature births

Neurologist Treats conditions and diseases of the brain, spinal cord, and nerves

Neurosurgeon Surgically treats conditions and diseases of the neurologic system

Obstetrician Treats women during pregnancy and postpartum

Oncologist Treats tumors (cancers) with surgical and medical methods

Ophthalmologist Treats conditions and diseases of the eye

Orthopedist Treats conditions and diseases of the muscles and bones

Otolaryngologist Treats conditions and diseases of the ears, nose, and throat

Pathologist Diagnoses conditions and diseases through changes in tissues

Pediatrician Treats conditions and diseases in children

Plastic surgeon Treats or restores structural conditions by corrective surgery

Podiatrist Treats conditions and diseases of the foot

Psychiatrist Treats mental disorders

Pulmonologist Medically treats conditions of the respiratory system

Radiologist Treats conditions and diseases with radiant energy

Rheumatologist Treats conditions and diseases of the muscles and joints

Surgeon Treats conditions and diseases with surgical methods

Thoracic surgeon Surgically treats conditions and diseases of the chest cavity

Urologist Treats conditions and diseases of the urinary and male reproductive systems

MEDICAL ORGANIZATIONS

AAD American Academy of Dermatology

AAI American Academy of Immunologists

AAN American Academy of Neurology

AANS American Association of Neurological Surgery (Surgeons)

AAO American Association of Ophthalmology (Orthodontists)

AAOG American Association of Obstetricians and Gynecologists

AAOO American Academy of Ophthalmology and Otolaryngology

AAOP American Academy of Oral Pathology

AAOS American Academy of Orthopaedic Surgeons

AAP American Academy of Pediatrics (Periodontology); Association of American Physicians

ACFO American College of Foot Orthopedists

ACFS American College of Foot Surgeons

ADA American Dermatological Association; American Diabetes (Dietetic) Association

AES American Epidemiological Society

AGA American Gastroenterological Association

AGS American Gynecological Society

AHA American Heart (Hospital) Association

ALPOS American Laryngological, Philological, and Otological Society

AMA American Medical Association

AMSUS Association of Military Surgeons of the United States

AMWA American Medical Women's (Writer's) Association

ANA American Neurological Association

AOA American Orthopedic (Osteopathic) Association

APA American Podiatry (Psychiatric) (Psychological) Association

AUA American Urological Association

NURSING SPECIALTIES

AD Associate degree nurse

A/NP Adult/nurse practitioner

BS (BSN) Bachelor of science (bachelor of science in nursing)

CCRN Critical care registered nurse

CEN Certified emergency nurse

CNM Certified nurse-midwife; clinical nurse manager

CNS Clinical nurse specialist

CRNA Certified registered nurse anesthetist

DN (ND) Doctorate in nursing (nursing doctor)

EdD Doctorate of education

FP-NP Family practice nurse practitioner

G-NP Geriatric nurse practitioner

LPN Licensed practical nurse

LVN Licensed vocational nurse

MEd Master of education

MPH Master of public health

MS (MSN) Master of science (master of science in nursing)

MSNR Master of science in nursing with research

NP Nurse practitioner

NP/C Nurse practitioner/certified

ONS Oncology nurse specialist

PhD Doctor of philosophy

PhDc Doctor of philosophy, candidate

P-NP Pediatric nurse practitioner

RN Registered nurse

RNA Registered nurse anesthetist

RNC Registered nurse certified

TNCC Trauma nurse core course

NURSING ORGANIZATIONS

AAACN American Academy of Ambulatory Care Nursing

AACCN American Association of Critical Care Nurses

AACN American Association of Colleges of Nursing

AAHN American Association for the History of Nursing, Inc.

AALNC American Association of Legal Nurse Consultants

AAMN American Assembly for Men in Nursing

AANA American Association of Nurse Anesthetists; American Association of Nurse Attorneys

AANN American Association of Neuroscience Nurses

AANP American Academy of Nurse Practitioners

AAOH American Association of Occupational Health Nurses, Inc.

AAON American Association of Office Nurses

AASPIN American Association of Spinal Cord Injury Nurses

ABNF Association of Black Nursing Faculty, Inc.

ACCH Association for the Care of Children's Health

ACHNE Association of Community Health Nursing Educators

ACHSA American Correctional Health Services Association

ACNM American College of Nurse Midwives

ACPN Advocates for Child Psychiatric Nursing

ACS American Cancer Society

AHA American Heart Association

AHNA American Holistic Nurses Association

ANA American Nurses Association

AN-Aids Association of Nurses in AIDS Care

ANC Army Nurse Corps

ANF American Nurses Foundation

ANNA American Nephrology Nurses' Association

AONE American Organization of Nurse Executives

AORN Association of Operating Room Nurses

APH American Public Health Association

APIC Association for Practitioners in Infection Control

APON Association of Pediatric Oncology Nurses

ARC American Red Cross

ARN Association of Rehabilitation Nurses

ASORN American Society of Ophthalmic Registered Nurses, Inc.

ASPAN American Society of Post Anesthesia Nurses

ASPRSN American Society of Plastic and Reconstructive Surgical Nurses, Inc.

ATDNF Alpha Tau Delta National Fraternity for Professional Nurses

ATS American Thoracic Society

AUAA American Urological Association Allied, Inc.

AWHONN Association of Women's Health, Obstetric, and Neonatal Nurses

CEP Chi Eta Phi Sorority, Inc.

CGEAN Council on Graduate Education for Administration in Nursing

CGFNS Commission on Graduates of Foreign Nursing Schools

CHA Catholic Health Association of the U.S.

CNA Canadian Nurses' Association

DANA Drug and Alcohol Nursing Association, Inc.

DDNA Developmental Disabilities Nurses Association

DNA Dermatology Nurses Association

ENA Emergency Nurses Association

FNIF Florence Nightingale International Foundation

FNS Frontier Nursing Service

ICLRN Interagency Council on Library Resources for Nursing

INS Intravenous Nurses Society

NADNA National Association of Directors of Nursing in Long-Term Care

NAHC National Association of Home Care
NAHCR National Association for Health Care
Recruitment
NAHN National Association of Hispanic Nurses
NANDA North American Nursing Diagnosis
Association
NANN National Association of Neonatal Nurses
NANP National Alliance of Nurse Practitioners
NANPRH National Association of Nurse
Practitioners in Reproductive Health
NAON National Association of Orthopaedic Nurses,
Inc.
NAPN National Association of Physician Nurses
NAPNAP National Association of Pediatric Nurse
Associates and Practitioners
NAPNES National Association for Practical Nurse
Education and Service
NASN National Association of School Nurses
NBNA National Black Nurses Association, Inc.
NCCDN National Consortium of Chemical
Dependency Nurses
NCF Nurses Christian Fellowship
NCSBON National Council of State Boards of
Nursing, Inc.
NEF Nurses Educational Funds, Inc.
NEHW Nurses Environmental Health Watch
NFLPN National Federation of Licensed Practical
Nurses, Inc.
NFNA National Flight Nurses Association
NFSNO National Federation of Specialty Nursing
Organizations
NGNA National Gerontological Nursing Association
NHPA Nurse Healers Professional Associates
NLN National League for Nursing
NMCHC National Maternal and Child Health
Clearinghouse
NNBA National Nurses in Business Association

NNSA National Nurses Society on Addictions

NNSDO National Nursing Staff Development
Organization

NOADN National Organization for Associate
Degree Nurses

NONPF National Organization of Nurse Practitioner
Faculties

NOVA Nurse Organization of Veterans Affairs

NOWWN National Organization of World War
Nurses

NSNA National Student Nurses' Association

ONS Oncology Nursing Society

RANCA Retired Army Nurse Corps Association

RNS Respiratory Nursing Society

SERPMHN Society for Education and Research in
Psychiatric Mental Health Nursing

SGNA Society of Gastroenterology Nurses and
Associates, Inc.

SOHEN Society of Otorhinolaryngology and
Head/Neck Nurses

SPN Society of Pediatric Nurses

SRAFN Society of Retired Air Force Nurses, Inc.

SRS Society of Rogerian Scholars

SVN Society for Vascular Nursing

TNS Transcultural Nursing Society

VNAA Visiting Nurse Association of America

BODY REGIONS

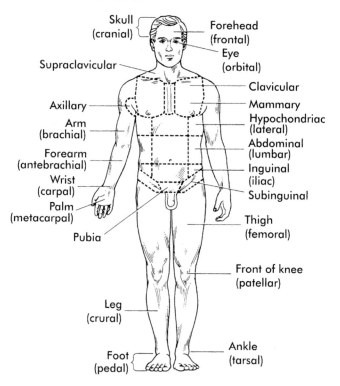

Figure 1-1   Body regions: anterior. (Modified from Austrin MG, Austrin HR: *Learning medical terminology*, ed 9, St Louis, 1998, Mosby.)

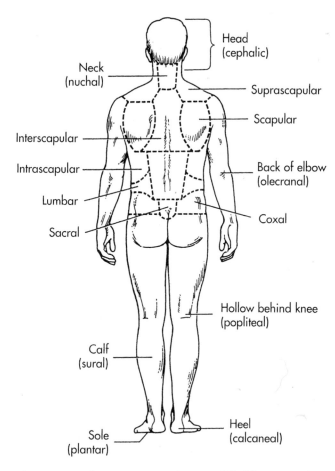

Figure 1-2 Body regions: posterior. (Modified from Austrin MG, Austrin HR: *Learning medical terminology,* ed 9, St Louis, 1998, Mosby.)

DIRECTIONS AND PLANES

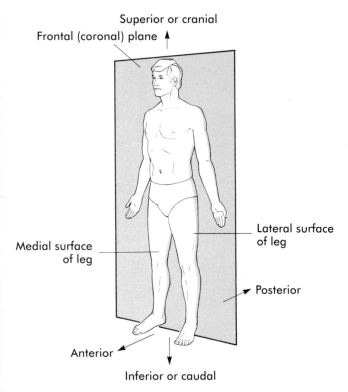

Figure 1-3 Frontal and lateral planes. (Modified from Austrin MG, Austrin HR: *Learning medical terminology,* ed 9, St Louis, 1998, Mosby.)

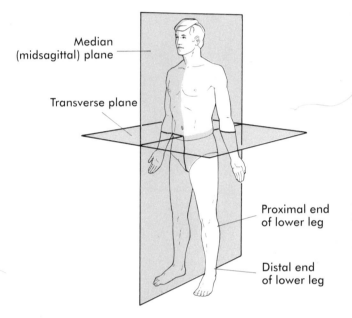

Figure 1-4   Median and transverse planes. (Modified from Austrin MG, Austrin HR: *Learning medical terminology,* ed 9, St Louis, 1998, Mosby.)

Chapter 2

Medications: Calculations and Administration

For an in-depth study of medications, calculations, and administration, consult the following publications:

Clark JF, Queener SF, Karb VB: *Pharmacologic basis of nursing practice,* ed 5, St Louis, 1997, Mosby.

Clayton BC, Stock YN: *Basic pharmacology for nurses,* ed 12, St Louis, 2001, Mosby.

Potter PA, Perry AG: *Fundamentals of nursing,* ed 5, St Louis, 2001, Mosby.

Skidmore-Roth L: *Mosby's 2002 nursing drug reference,* St Louis, 2002 Mosby.

EQUIVALENT MEASURES
Metric System

To change from a larger to a smaller unit, MULTIPLY the number by 10, 100, etc., or move the decimal point to the RIGHT. To change from a smaller to larger unit, DIVIDE the number by 10, 100, etc., or move the decimal to the LEFT.

Weight

1 kilogram (kg/Kg) = 1000 grams (gm)
1 gram (Gm/gm/g/G) = 1000 milligrams (mg)
1 milligram (mg) = 1000 micrograms (mcg)

Volume

1 liter (L) = 1000 milliliters (ml)
1 deciliter (dl) = 100 milliliters (ml)
1 milliliter (ml) = 1 cubic centimeter (cc)

Length

1 meter (m) = 100 centimeters (cm)
1 meter (m) = 1000 millimeters (mm)
1 centimeter (cm) = 10 millimeters (mm)

Apothecary System

Weight: grains (gr); volume: minims (m), drams (dr), ounces (oz)

Metric-to-Apothecary Conversions

Grams to grains: Multiply grams (gm) by 15
Milligrams to grains: Divide milligrams (mg) by 60

Apothecary-to-Metric Conversions

Grains to grams: Divide grains (gr) by 15
Grains to milligrams: Multiply grains (gr) by 60

Household System

Weight
1 tablespoon (tbsp/T) = 3 teaspoons (tsp/t)
1 cup (c) = 16 tablespoons (tbsp/T)
1 pound (lb) = 16 ounces (oz)

Volume
1 gallon (gal) = 4 quarts (qt)
1 quart (qt) = 2 pints (pt)
1 pint (pt) = 2 cups (c)
1 cup (c) = 8 ounces (oz)
30cc = 1 ounce (oz)

Kilogram-to-Pound Conversions
Kilograms to pounds: Multiply kilograms (kg) by 2.2
Pounds to kilograms: Divide pounds (lb) by 2.2

Household-Metric Conversions
15 drops (gtt) = 1 ml
1 tsp/t = 4-5 ml
1 tbsp/T = 16 ml
1 cup/c = 240 ml
1 pint/pt = ≈480 ml
1 quart/qt = ≈960 ml
1 gallon/gal = ≈3840 ml or 5 L

PEDIATRIC BODY SURFACE AREA

$$\text{Child's dose} = \frac{\text{Child's body surface area (BSA)}}{1.7}$$

CALCULATING STRENGTH OF A SOLUTION

Solution strength: Desired solution:

$$\frac{X}{100} = \frac{\text{Amount of drug desired}}{\text{Amount of finished solution}}$$

CALCULATING IV DRIP RATES

The *drops per 1 ml* is the number of drops needed to fill a 1-ml syringe.

The *rate* is the number of milliliters per hour.

The *drip rate* is the amount of volume divided by the time needed to infuse.

Following is the equation that can be used to calculate IV drip rates:

$$\frac{\text{Total volume}}{\text{Total time}} = \frac{\text{ml}}{1 \text{ minute}} \times \frac{\text{No. of gtt}}{\text{ml}} = \frac{\text{Drops}}{\text{Minute}}$$

Microdrops: A Simple Calculation

10 drops or gtt: ml/hr = gtt/min per micro divided by 6

15 drops or gtt: ml/hr = gtt/min per micro divided by 4

20 drops or gtt: ml/hr = gtt/min per micro divided by 3

60 drops or gtt/ml: ml/hr = gtt/min

DRUG ADMINISTRATION
Routes of Administration
Oral (PO), sublingual (SL), buccal (B), rectal (PR), topical (T), subcutaneous (SC or SQ), intradermal (ID), intramuscular (IM), intravenous (IV), inhalation (IH), transdermal patch (TD), intrathecal (IT), intraosseous (IO), intraperitoneal (IP), intrapleural (IPL), and intraarterial (IA).

Six Rights
Client, drug, dose, time, route, documentation.

Types of Drug Preparations
Aerosol spray, capsule (coated), cream (non-greasy), elixir (alcohol), extract (concentrated), gel (clear, semisolid), liniment (oily), lotion, lozenge, ointment (semisolid), paste (thicker than ointment), pills, powder (ground drug), spirit (alcohol), suppository (dissolves at body temperature), syrup (sugar based), tablet (coated), tincture (diluted alcohol), transdermal (absorbed).

Therapeutic Drugs
Palliative gives relief; *example:* pain medications.
Curative cures disease; *example:* antibiotics.
Supportive helps body's functions; *example:* blood pressure medications.
Destructive destroys cells; *example:* chemotherapy.
Restorative returns to health; *example:* vitamins.

Common Allergic Responses
Difficulty breathing, palpitations, skin rashes, nausea, vomiting, pruritus, rhinitis, tearing, wheezing, diarrhea. *Report all allergic responses.*

COMMON DRUG TERMINOLOGY

Absorption The passage of drug molecules into the blood

Abuse A maladaptive pattern of drug usage

Allergic reaction An unpredictable response to a drug

Biotransformation Drug metabolism from active to inactive state

Classification Indicates the effect on a body system

Distribution How a drug is absorbed into the body tissues

Duration Length of time in the body

Excretion The exit of the drug from the body

Form Determines the routes of administration

Genetic difference The makeup by which a person's genetic background may affect the drug's actions in the body

Half-life Time of elimination from body

Idiosyncratic Drugs that are overactive or underactive

Interactions When one drug modifies the actions of another

Medication A substance used in the treatment, cure, relief, or prevention of disease

Onset First response of drug in the body

Peak Highest level of drug in the body

Pharmacokinetics The study of how drugs enter the body, reach their site of action, are metabolized, and exit the body

Physiologic variables The normal difference between men and women and differences in weight may affect the metabolism of a drug

Plateau Concentration of scheduled doses

Side effects Unintended secondary effects

Standards Guidelines for purity and quality of a drug
Therapeutic Beneficial level of drug
Tolerance Low response to a drug
Toxic Not beneficial or lethal level of drug
Trough Lowest level of drug in the body

Drug Dependence

A person may be considered dependent on a drug if he or she possesses at least three of the following qualities over a 12-month period:
- Consumes larger doses than intended
- Consumes drug for a longer time period than intended
- Frequent intoxication
- Withdrawal symptoms when away from substance
- Work or social activities are given up to consume more substance
- Continues to use substance despite information or warnings of harm
- Increased time is spent acquiring substances
- Marked tolerance for substance

Modified from American Psychiatric Association: *Diagnostic and statistical manual of mental disorders (DSM-IV)*, ed 4, Washington, DC, 1994, The Association.

Drug Actions in Older Adults		
Problem	**Cause**	**Intervention**
Difficulty swallowing medications	Loss of elasticity in oral mucosa	Have client rinse mouth before taking pills.
Erosion of esophageal tissues from pills	Delayed esophageal clearance	Position client upright. Crush pill (if possible).
Stomach irritation from medications	Decreased gastric acidity/peristalsis	Have client drink a full glass of water.
Slower drug absorption	Reduced colon muscle tone	Increase fluids. Avoid constipation.
Fragile veins	Reduced skin elasticity	Avoid IV punctures.
Slower drug metabolism	Reduced liver size	Monitor dosages.
	Reduced hepatic flow	Monitor liver effects.
Slower drug excretion	Reduced glomerular filtration	Monitor dosages. Monitor renal effects.

THERAPEUTIC DRUGS THAT REQUIRE SERUM DRUG LEVELS*†

Antibiotics
Amikacin (Amikin)
Gentamicin (Garamycin)
Netilmicin (Netromycin)
Tobramycin (Nebcin)
Vancomycin (Vancocin)

Anticonvulsants
Carbamazepine (Tegretol)
Phenobarbital
Phenytoin (Dilantin)
Primidone (Mysoline)
Valproic acid

Cardiovascular Drugs
Digoxin (Lanoxin)
Lidocaine (Xylocaine)
Procainamide (Pronestyl)
Quinidine

Respiratory Drug
Theophylline

Antirejection Drug
Cyclosporine

*Specific therapeutic blood levels may vary per facility.
†Other drugs may be included depending on the facility.

Compatibility Chart for Drugs in Syringe

	Atropine	Benzquinamide	Butorphanol	Chlorpromazine	Dimenhydrinate	Diphenhydramine	Droperidol	Fentanyl	Glycopyrrolate	Hydroxyzine
Atropine	■	C	C	C	C	C	C	C	C	C
Benzquinamide	C	■							C	C
Butorphanol	C		■		I	C	C	C		C
Chlorpromazine	C			■	I	C	C	C	C	C
Dimenhydrinate	C		I	I	■	C	C	C	I	I
Diphenhydramine	C		C	C	C	■	C	C	C	C
Droperidol	C		C	C	C	C	■	C	C	C
Fentanyl	C		C	C	C	C	C	■		C
Glycopyrrolate	C	C		C	I	C	C		■	C
Hydroxyzine	C	C	C	C	I	C	C	C	C	■
Meperidine	C	C	C	C	C	C	C	C	C	C
Metoclopramide	C		C	C	C	C	C	C		C
Midazolam	C	C	C	C	I	C	C	C	C	C
Morphine	C	C	C	C	C	C	C	C	C	C
Nalbuphine	C					C	C		C	C
Pentazocine	C	C	C	C	C	C	C	C	I	C
Pentobarbital	I	I	I	I	I	I	I	I	I	I
Perphenazine	C			C	C	C	C	C		
Prochlorperazine	C		C	C	I	C	C	C	C	C
Promazine	C			C	I	C	C	C	C	C
Promethazine	C		C	C	I	C	C	C	C	C
Scopolamine Hbr	C	I		C	C	C	C	C	C	C
Secobarbital	I	I		I			I	I		
Thiethylperazine										
Trimethobenzamide									C	

From Clark JF, Queener SF, Karb VB: *Pharmacologic basis of nursing practice,* ed 5, St Louis, 1997, Mosby.

	Meperidine	Metoclopramide	Midazolam	Morphine	Nalbuphine	Pentazocine	Pentobarbital	Perphenazine	Prochlorperazine	Promazine	Promethazine	Scopolamine Hbr	Secobarbital	Thiethylperazine	Trimethobenzamide
	C	C	C	C	C	C	I	C	C	C	C	C	I		
	C		C	C		C	I					C	I		
	C	C	C	C		C	I		C	C		C			
	C	C	C	C		C	I		C	C	C	C	C	I		
	C	C	I	C		C	I		C	I	I	I	C		
	C	C	C	C	C	C	I		C	C	C	C	C	I		
	C	C	C	C	C	C	I		C	C	C	C	C	I		
	C	C	C	C		C	I		C	C	C	C	C			
	C		C	C	C	I	I			C	C	C	C	I		C
	C	C	C	C	C	C	I			C	C	C	C			
	■	C	C	I		C	I	C	C	C	C	C			
	C	■	C	C		C		C	C	C	C	C	I		
	C	C	■	C	C		I	I	I	C	C	C		C	C
	I	C	C	■		C	#	C	#	C	#	C			
		C			■		I		C	#	#	C			C
	C	C		C		■	I	C	C	C	C	C	I		
	I		I	#	I	I	■	I	I	I	I	C			
	C	C	I	C		C	I	■	C		C	C		I	
	C	C	I	#	C	C	I	C	■	C	C	C	I		
	C	C	C	C	#	C	I		C	■	C	C	I		
	C	C	C	#	#	C	I	C	C	C	■	C			
	C	C	C	C	C	C	C	C	C	C	C	■			
	I				I				I	I			■		
		C					C							■	
		C		C											■

C, Compatible if used within 15 minutes; *I*, incompatible; #, compatibility varies with brand and dilution (check with pharmacist); □, no documented information.

ADMINISTRATION TECHNIQUES

Injection Guide for Needle Size and Volume		
		Volume Injected (ml)
	Needle Sizes	Average	Range
Intradermal	26 or 27 gauge × 3/8 in	0.1	0.001-1.0
Subcutaneous	25-27 gauge × 1/2 to 5/8 in	0.5	0.5-1.5
Intramuscular			
Gluteus medius	20-23 gauge × 1 1/2 to 3 in	2-4	1-5
Gluteus minimus	20-23 gauge × 1 1/2 to 3 in	1-4	1-5
Vastus lateralis	22-25 gauge × 5/8 to 1 1/2 in	1-4	1-5
Deltoid	23-25 gauge × 5/8 to 1 in	0.5	0.5-2
Intravenous bolus	18-23 gauge × 1 to 1 1/2 in	1-10	0.5-50 (or more by continuous infusion)

From Clark JB, Queener SF, Karb VB: *Pharmacologic basis of nursing practice*, ed 5, St Louis, 1997, Mosby.

Flushing Venous Access Devices

Device	Solution/Volume	Frequency
Peripheral capped line	Normal saline (2-5 ml)	q 8 hours or after use and before use
Hickman or CVP	Heparinized saline 10 units/ml (5 ml)	qd or after each use
PICC or Cook catheter	Heparinized saline 10 units/ml (5 ml)	qd or after each use
Groshong catheter	Normal saline (10 ml) (20 ml w/viscous med/blood)	q week or after each use
Groshong implanted	Normal saline (10 ml)	q monthly
Per-Q-Catheter	Heparinized saline 10 units/ml (5 ml)	qd or after each use

Continued

Flushing Venous Access Devices—cont'd		
Device	**Solution/Volume**	**Frequency**
Gesco catheter	Heparinized saline 10 units/ml (5 ml)	qd or after each use
Midline-L/Luther Cath (should not use for blood draws)	Heparinized saline 10 units/ml (5 ml)	qd or after each use
Implanted port (chest)	Huber-type needle Heparinized saline 100 units/ml (5 ml)	q month or after each use
PAS port (arm)	Heparinized saline 10 units/ml (5 ml) Normal saline (20 ml)	qd or after each use After blood draws

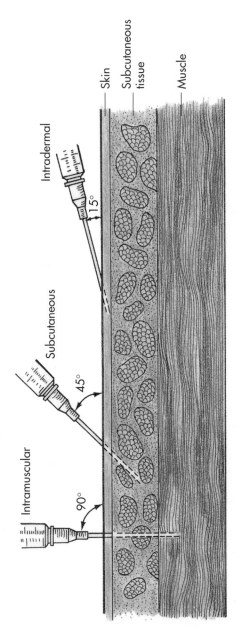

Figure 2-1 Comparison of the angles of insertion of intramuscular, subcutaneous, and intradermal injections. (From Potter PA, Perry AG: *Fundamentals of nursing: concepts, process, and practice,* ed 5, St Louis, 2000, Mosby.)

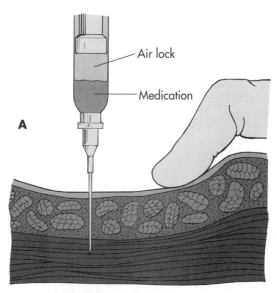

During Injection

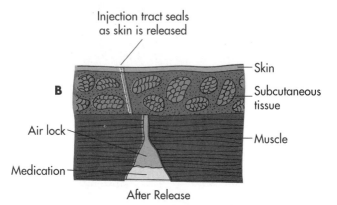

After Release

Figure 2-2 **A,** Pull on overlying skin during intramuscular injection moves tissues to prevent later tracking. **B,** Z track left after injection prevents deposit of medication through sensitive tissue. (From Potter PA, Perry AG: *Fundamentals of nursing,* ed 5, St Louis, 2001, Mosby.)

INJECTION SITES

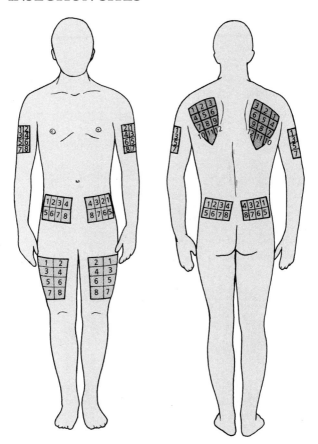

Figure 2-3   Common sites used for subcutaneous injections. (From Potter PA, Perry AG: *Fundamentals of nursing,* ed 5, St Louis, 2001, Mosby.)

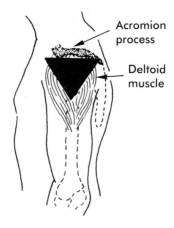

Figure 2-4 Deltoid injections. (From Clark JB, Queener SF, Karb VB: *Pharmacologic basis of nursing practice,* ed 5, St Louis, 1997, Mosby.)

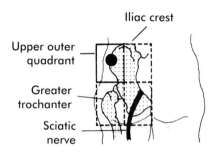

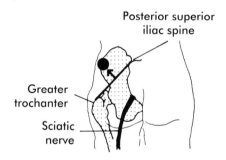

Figure 2-5 Dorsogluteal injections. (From Clark JB, Queener SF, Karb VB: *Pharmacologic basis of nursing practice,* ed 5, St Louis, 1997, Mosby.)

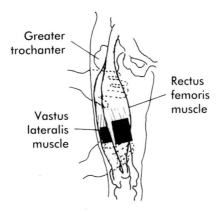

Figure 2-6 Vastus lateralis injections. (From Clark JB, Queener SF, Karb VB: *Pharmacologic basis of nursing practice,* ed 5, St Louis, 1997, Mosby.)

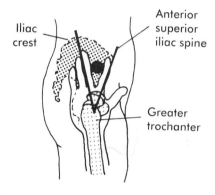

Figure 2-7 Ventrogluteal injections. (From Clark JB, Queener SF, Karb VB: *Pharmacologic basis of nursing practice,* ed 5, St Louis, 1997, Mosby.)

Chapter 3

 # Infection Control

For an in-depth study of infection control, consult the following publications:

Hospital Infection Control Practices Advisory Committee, Centers for Disease Control and Prevention: *Guidelines for isolation precautions in hospitals,* Washington, DC, 1996, Public Health Service, US Department of Health and Human Services.

Potter PA, Perry AG: *Fundamentals of nursing,* ed 5, St Louis, 2001, Mosby.

Universal precautions for prevention of transmission of human immuno-deficiency virus, hepatitis B virus, and other bloodborne pathogens in health care settings, *MMWR Morbid Mortal Wkly Rep* 37(Suppl 24): 377, 1988.

BASIC TERMS

Asepsis Prevention of the transfer of microorganisms and pathogens

Chain Path of infection; the components of the infectious disease process

Clean Presence of few microorganisms or pathogens with no visible debris

Colonization Presence of a potentially infectious organism in or on a host but not causing disease

Communicable Ability of a microorganism to spread disease

Contamination Presence of an infectious agent on a surface

Dirty Presence of many microorganisms or pathogens; any soiled item

Disease Alteration of normal tissues, body processes, or functions

Etiology Cause of a disease

Immunity Resistance to a disease associated with the presence of antibodies

Infection Invasion of tissues by a disease-causing microorganism(s)

Medical asepsis Measures that limit pathologic spread of microorganisms

Nosocomial infection A hospital-acquired infection (not present or incubating on admission)

Ports How microorganisms exit and enter a system

Reservoir Storage place for organisms to grow

Source Point that initiates chain of infection

Sterile Absence of all microorganisms

Surgical asepsis Measures to keep pathogenic organisms at a minimum during surgery

Transmission Method by which microorganisms travel from one host to another

Virulence Ability of a microorganism to produce disease

STAGES OF INFECTION

Incubation From initial contact with infectious
  material to onset of symptoms

Prodrome From nonspecific signs and symptoms to
  specific signs and symptoms (prodromal)

Illness Presence of specific signs and symptoms

Convalescence During the recovery period, as
  symptoms subside

THE INFLAMMATORY PROCESS

Stage I

Constriction of blood vessels, dilatation of small vessels, increased vessel permeability; increased leukocytes; swelling and pain. Leukocytes begin to engulf the infection.

Stage II

Exudation with fluids and dead cells.

Serous Clear; part of the blood

Purulent Thick; pus with leukocytes

Sanguineous Bloody

Stage III

Repair of tissues. Examples include:

Regeneration Same tissues

Stroma Connective tissues

Parenchyma Functional part

Fibrous Scar

SUMMARY OF ISOLATION PRECAUTIONS

Hand washing Should be done before and after working with all clients and after removing gloves; immediately if hands become contaminated with blood or other body fluids

Gloves Should be worn whenever contact with body fluids is likely

Mask and/or eye cover Should be worn when splashing of body fluids is likely

Gown Should be worn when soiling of exposed skin or clothing is likely

CPR Should be done with pocket masks or mechanical ventilation, avoiding mouth to mouth

Needles Should not be recapped unless using the one-handed method
CAUTION: *Do not break needles; discard all sharp objects immediately.*

Private rooms Should be used whenever possible

Spills Should be cleaned immediately with bleach and water (one part bleach to nine parts water) for FDA-approved cleaning agent

Specimens Should be collected in leakproof, puncture-resistant container; outside of container must be free of contaminants

Transporting clients Should be kept to a minimum when working with infected clients

TYPES OF ISOLATION PRECAUTIONS
Standard Precautions
- Used to help prevent nosocomial infections.
- Used when working with all clients.
- To replace the universal precautions and the blood and body precautions.
- Applies to blood, all body fluids, secretions, excretions (except sweat).
- To be used even if blood is not visible.
- Also applies to nonintact skin and mucous membranes.
- Designed to reduce the risk of transmission of microorganisms.

Transmission-Based Precautions
- Used for clients known or suspected to be infected with specific pathogens.
- There are three subgroups of transmission-based precautions.
- Subgroups can be combined for diseases with multiple transmissions routes.
- Subgroups are to be used in addition to standard precautions.

Airborne Precautions
- Used for airborne infectious agents of 5 μm or smaller.

Droplet Precautions
- Used for infectious agents larger than 5 μm.
- Droplets from the mucous membranes of the nose or mouth.
- Droplets from coughing, sneezing, talking.
- Droplet contracted within 3 feet or less.

Contact Precautions

Contact can be direct or indirect:

- Direct is skin-to-skin contact through touch, turning, bathing.
- Indirect contact is made by touching contaminated items, items within the client's room.

MRSA AND VRE

MRSA (methicillin-resistant *Staphylococcus aureus*)
VRE (vancomycin-resistant *Enterococcus*)
These are two of the most difficult infections to treat.
USE **CONTACT PRECAUTIONS** for a skin or body
   fluid, MRSA, or VRE infection.
USE **DROPLET PRECAUTIONS** for a respiratory
   MRSA infection.
When MRSA is found in tracheal secretions.

MRSA Precautions

Masks Necessary if client's respiratory tract is colo-
   nized or has an active infection. Must use when
   suctioning, or when client has a productive
   cough.
Gowns Necessary if in contact with secretions.
Gloves Necessary for all contact with items that
   may be contaminated.
Other Good hand washing with chlorhexidine
   gluconate soap.
**Always wash hands before entering and after
leaving client's room.**

VRE Precautions

Masks Necessary if contact with secretions is likely.
Gowns Necessary if contact with secretions is likely.
Gloves Necessary for all contact with items that
   may be contaminated.
Other Good hand washing with chlorhexidine glu-
   conate soap.
**Always wash hands before entering and after
leaving client's room.**

COMMON BACTERIA*

Ear *Corynebacterium,* diphtheroids, saprophytes, *Staphylococcus, Streptococcus*

Esophagus/stomach None; usually microorganisms from the mouth or food

Eye *Corynebacterium, Enterobacter, Haemophilus, Moraxella, Neisseria, Staphylococcus, Streptococcus*

Genitalia *Bacteroides, Candida albicans, Corynebacterium,* enterococcus, *Fusobacterium, Mycobacterium, Mycoplasma, Neisseria, Staphylococcus, Streptococcus*

Ileum (lower) *Bacteroides, Clostridium, Enterobacter,* enterococcus, *Lactobacillus, Mycobacterium, Staphylococcus*

Ileum (upper) Enterococcus, *Lactobacillus*

Large intestine *Acinetobacter, Actinomyces, Alcaligenes, Bacteroides, Clostridium, Enterobacter,* enterococcus, *Eubacterium, Fusobacterium, Mycobacterium, Peptococcus, Peptostreptococcus*

Mouth *Actinomyces, Bacteroides, Candida albicans, Corynebacterium, Enterobacter, Fusobacterium, Lactobacillus, Peptococcus, Peptostreptococcus, Staphylococcus, Streptococcus, Torulopsis, Veillonella*

Nose *Corynebacterium, Enterobacter, Haemophilus, Moraxella, Neisseria, Staphylococcus, Streptococcus*

Oropharynx *Corynebacterium, Enterobacter, Haemophilus, Staphylococcus, Streptococcus*

Skin *Bacillus, Candida albicans, Corynebacterium,* dermatophytes, *Enterobacter, Peptococcus, Propionibacterium acnes, Staphylococcus, Streptococcus*

*Normal flora found on or in the body.

TUBERCULOSIS
Agent
Mycobacterium tuberculosis
Bovine TB (*Mycobacterium bovis*), which is transmitted through cattle and unpasteurized milk

Reservoir
Primarily humans, diseased cattle, badgers, and other small mammals

Mode of Transmission
Spread by respiratory droplets
Direct invasion through mucous membranes

Incubation
4 to 12 weeks
Subsequent risk of pulmonary infection is greatest within the first year
Infections may persist for a lifetime

Prevention
Education regarding the mode of transmission and early diagnosis
Monitoring of groups at risk (people who are HIV positive, recent immigrants, homeless people, people residing in crowded, substandard housing)
Report new cases for public health follow-up
Implement standard precautions and transmission-based airborne precautions immediately with any suspected cases (see p. 63)
Eliminate tuberculosis among dairy cattle
Pasteurize milk

OVERVIEW OF COMMON INFECTIOUS DISEASES*†

AIDS

Transmission through blood and body fluids, sexual contact, sharing IV needles, contaminated blood, and from mother to fetus.

Considerations. Education regarding mode of transmission, avoidance of sexual contact with infected persons, use of latex condoms, proper blood screening of all transfusable products, and proper handling of needles and other contaminated material.

Chickenpox/Herpes Zoster Virus (Varicella/Shingles)

Transmission through respiratory droplets or by direct contact with open lesions.

Considerations. Strict isolation, avoidance of direct contact with lesions, and administration of varicella-zoster immune globulin. Caregivers should be chickenpox immune.

Chlamydia

Transmission through sexual contact.

Considerations. Public education, use of latex condoms.

German Measles (Rubella)

Transmission through respiratory droplets.

Considerations. Education regarding vaccines and prenatal care, avoidance of contact.

---

*Standard precautions are required for all persons with infectious diseases (see pp. 63-64).
†Check state requirements for reporting infectious diseases.

Gonorrhea
Transmission through vaginal secretions, semen, sexual contact.

Considerations. Public education regarding mode of transmission, use of latex condoms.

Hepatitis A and Hepatitis E
Transmission through direct contact with water, food, or feces.

Considerations. Hand washing before touching food, proper water and sewage treatment, reporting of cases, immunoglobulin vaccination when traveling to high-risk areas, proper disposal of contaminants.

Hepatitis B
Transmission through all fluids of an infected source.

Considerations. Hepatitis B vaccination, public education, blood screening, use of gloves when handling secretions, proper sterilization of equipment, reporting of all known cases to disease control centers.

Hepatitis C
Transmission through contaminated blood, plasma, and needles.

Considerations. See Hepatitis B.

Hepatitis D
Hepatitis D can develop only in those individuals who have active Hepatitis B or in those people who are carriers of Hepatitis D.

Measles (Red, Hard, Morbilli, Rubeola)
Transmission through airborne droplets or direct contact with lesions.

Considerations. Public education about vaccine, avoidance of contact with infected persons.

Meningitis (Bacterial)
Transmission through airborne droplets or direct contact.

Considerations. Public education, vaccination, early prophylaxis of exposed contacts.

Mononucleosis
Transmission through saliva.

Considerations. Public education, good hygiene.

Mumps
Transmission through airborne droplets and saliva.

Considerations. Vaccination.

Pneumonia
Transmission through airborne droplets.

Considerations. Vaccination, good hygiene.

Polio (Poliomyelitis)
Transmission through oral or fecal contact.

Considerations. Vaccination.

Salmonellosis
Transmission through ingestion of contaminated food.

Considerations. Proper cooking and storage of food, good hand washing before food preparation.

Syphilis
Transmission through sexual contact, direct contact with lesions, and blood transfusions.

Considerations. Public education regarding transmission, prenatal screening, and prenatal follow-up; use of latex condoms, blood screening.

Tetanus (Lockjaw)
Transmission through direct contact of wounds with infected soil or feces.

Considerations. Public education regarding mode of transmission, vaccination.

Tuberculosis
Transmission through airborne droplets; bovine TB through unpasteurized milk.

Considerations. Public education and screening, improvement of overcrowded living conditions, and pasteurization of milk.

Typhoid Fever
Transmission through contaminated water, urine, or feces.

Considerations. Good hygiene, sanitary water, proper sewage care, and vaccinations.

Whooping Cough (Pertussis)

Transmission through airborne droplets and nasal discharge.

Considerations. Vaccination, wearing of masks when near infected clients, reporting of all cases.

FACTS ABOUT INFLUENZA FOR ADULTS*

- Influenza can be prevented by the use of an effective vaccine.
- A person cannot catch influenza from a vaccine.
- Influenza in conjunction with pneumonia is the sixth leading cause of death in the United States among older adults.
- Because influenza viruses can change from year to year, an annual influenza shot is needed each fall.
- The best time to receive an influenza shot is October through December.
- Influenza shots will not protect you from other illnesses, such as colds, bronchitis, and the stomach influenza or gastritis. These three illnesses are often called "the flu."
- Vaccinations can prevent up to 50% of the 140,000 hospitalizations and 80% of the 300,000 deaths that occur each year.
- The influenza vaccine is fully paid for by Medicare Part B.
- Influenza can worsen heart and lung disease and diabetes and can lead to pneumonia.

*Modified from the National Coalition for Adult Immunization: *Facts about influenza and pneumococcal disease*, Bethesda, Md, 1998, The Coalition.

FACTS ABOUT PNEUMOCOCCAL DISEASE FOR ADULTS*

- Pneumococcal disease can be prevented by the use of an effective vaccine.
- A person cannot catch pneumococcal disease from a vaccine.
- Pneumococcal disease in conjunction with influenza is the fifth leading cause of death in the United States.
- The pneumococcal vaccine is fully paid for by Medicare Part B.
- The vaccine can be given any time of the year and can be given with the influenza vaccine.

*Modified from the National Coalition for Adult Immunization: *Facts about influenza and pneumococcal disease,* Bethesda, Md, 1998, The Coalition.

Specimen Collection Techniques

Amount Needed*	Collection Device	Specimen Collection and Transport
Wound Culture		
As much as possible (after cleaning skin to remove flora)	Sterile cotton-tipped swab or syringe	Place sterile test tube or culturette tube on clean paper towel. After swabbing center of wound site, grasp collection tube by holding it with paper towel. Carefully insert swab without touching outside of tube. After washing hands and securing tube's top, transfer labeled tube into bag for transport to laboratory.

Blood Culture

10 ml per culture bottle, from two different venipuncture sites (volume may differ based on collection containers)	Syringes and culture media bottles	Perform venipuncture at two different sites to decrease likelihood of both specimens being contaminated by skin flora. Wash hands. Inject 10 ml of blood into each bottle. Secure tops of bottles, label specimens, and send to laboratory.

Stool Culture

Small amount, approximately the size of a walnut	Clean cup with seal top (not necessary to be sterile) and tongue blade	Using tongue blade, collect needed amount of feces from bedpan. Transfer feces to cup without touching cup's outside surface. Wash hands, and place seal on cup. Label specimen. Transfer specimen cup into clean bag for transport to laboratory.

Continued

From Potter PA, Perry AG: *Fundamentals of nursing*, ed 5, St Louis, 2001, Mosby.
*Agency policies may differ on type of containers, amount of specimen material required, and bagging.

Specimen Collection Techniques—cont'd

Amount Needed*	Collection Device	Specimen Collection and Transport
Urine Culture		
1-5 ml	Syringe and sterile cup	Using syringe to collect specimen if client has Foley catheter. Have client follow procedure to obtain clean-voided specimen if not catheterized. Transfer urine into sterile container by injecting urine from syringe or pouring it from used container. Wash hands and secure top of labeled container. Transfer labeled specimen into clean bag for transport to laboratory.

From Potter PA, Perry AG: *Fundamentals of nursing*, ed 5, St Louis, 2001, Mosby.
*Agency policies may differ on type of containers, amount of specimen material required, and bagging.

TYPES OF IMMUNITY

Active Antibodies produced in body; long lasting

    Natural Antibodies produced during an active infection

    Examples: Chickenpox, mumps, measles

    Artificial Vaccines of actual antigens

    Examples: Mumps, measles, rubella (MMR)

Passive Antibodies produced outside the body; short acting

    Natural Antibodies passed from mother to child through placenta and breast milk

    Artificial Injected immune serum

ANTIBODY FUNCTIONS

IgM First to respond; activates the complement system; stimulates ingestion by macrophage; principal antibody of the blood

IgG Most prevalent antibody; major antibody of the tissues; produced after IgM; only antibody to cross placenta; antitoxin; antiviral

IgA Principal antibody of the GI tract; found in tears, saliva, sweat, breast milk; protects epithelial lining

IgD Only in minute concentrations; function unknown

IgE For allergic reactions

Chapter 4

Basic Nursing Assessments

For an in-depth study of basic nursing assessments,
consult the following publications:

AJN/Mosby: *Nursing boards review for the NCLEX-RN examination,* ed 10,
    St Louis, 1996, Mosby.
Austrin MG, Austin HR: *Learning medical terminology,* ed 9, St Louis, 1998,
    Mosby.
Lewis SM, Collier IC, Heitkemper MM: *Medical-surgical nursing,* ed 5,
    St Louis, 2000, Mosby.
Potter PA: *Pocket guide to health assessment,* ed 4, St Louis, 1998, Mosby.
Potter PA, Perry AG: *Fundamentals of nursing,* ed 5, St Louis, 2001, Mosby.

THE CLIENT INTERVIEW
Demographics
Includes name, address, sex, age, birth date, marital status or significant other, religion, race, education, occupation, hobbies, significant life events.

Past Health History
Includes history of smoking, heart disease, alcohol or other drug use or abuse, surgeries, injuries, childhood diseases and vaccinations, hypertension, diabetes, arthritis, seizures, cancer, emotional problems, transfusions, drug or food allergies, perception of client's health or illness, lifestyle, hygiene and eating habits, health practices.

Past Family Medical History
Includes history of heart disease, alcohol or drug use or abuse, diabetes, arthritis, cancer, emotional problems.

Current Situation
Reasons for seeking help or chief complaint; include annual check-up, follow-up care, second opinion, new symptoms, monitoring existing health problem(s).

History of Present Illness
Includes location and quality of symptoms, chronology, aggravating and alleviating factors, associated symptoms, effect on lifestyle, measures used to deal with symptoms, review of body systems.

FUNCTIONAL ASSESSMENT
Health Perceptions
General health (good, fair, poor)
Tobacco/alcohol use (how much, how long)
Recreational or prescribed medications (list)
Hygiene practices

Nutrition
Type of diet (list)
Enjoys snacks (yes/no, what type)
Fluid intake (types of fluids)
Fluid restriction (yes/no)
Skin (normal, dry, rash)
Teeth (own, dentures, bridge)
Weight (recent gain or loss)

Respiration/Circulation
Respiratory problems (shortness of breath)
Smoking history
Circulation problems (chest pain, edema, pacemaker)

Elimination
Upper GI (nausea, vomiting, dysphagia, discomfort)
Bowels (frequency, consistency, last bowel movement, ostomy)
Bladder (incontinence, dysuria, urgency, frequency, nocturia, hematuria)

Activity/Exercise
Energy level (high, normal, low)
Usual exercise/activity patterns (recent changes)
Needs assistance with (eating, bathing, dressing)
Requirements (cane, walker, wheelchair, crutches)

Sleep
Problems (falling asleep, early waking, hours per
   night, napping)
Methods used to facilitate sleep
Feelings on waking (fatigued, refreshed)

Cognitive
Educational level
Learning needs
Communication barriers (list)
Memory loss (yes/no)
Developmental age
Reads English (yes/no)
Other languages (list)

Sensory
Hearing/vision (no problems, impaired, devices)
Pain (yes/no, how managed)

Coping/Stress
Needs (social services, financial counselor)
May need (home care, nursing home)
Coping mechanisms used by client

Self-Perception
How illness/wellness is affecting patient
Body image or self-esteem concerns

Role/Relationships
Significant other or emergency contacts
Primary, secondary, or tertiary roles
Role changes caused by illness/wellness
Role conflicts caused by illness/wellness

Sexuality

Last menstrual period, menopause, breast examination

Testicular examination

How illness may affect sexuality

How hospitalization may affect sexuality

Any questions, needs, or additional concerns

Values/Beliefs

Religious or cultural affiliation

Religious or cultural beliefs concerning health or illness

Holiday or food restrictions while hospitalized

Religious or cultural restrictions on medications or treatments

Religious or cultural rituals needed while hospitalized

Clergy or religious leader requested while hospitalized

CULTURAL ASSESSMENT

Include introductory information, such as:
- Client's name, unit, or room number
- Admission date, admitting diagnosis
- Proposed length of stay

Information about the country can be important:
- What is the cultural or ethnic affiliation?
- In what country was the client born?
- How many years has he or she been in the United States?
- What generation American is the client?

Assess language needs:
- Does the client need an interpreter (what language)?
- Does the client need a communication tool (language board)?
- Could the client use the ATT language line (available through most local telephone companies)?

Assess for cultural practices:
- Are there special rituals that may need to be honored?
- Are there special health practices that may need to be honored?
- How will the illness affect cultural practices?
- How will the illness affect cultural rituals?

Assess for cultural supports:
- Which cultural or ethnic supports may help your client?
- To whom does the client turn for help?
- How does the client describe his or her family?
- Who is the client's main source of support?
- Who is the client's main source of hope?

SPIRITUAL ASSESSMENT

Include introductory information, such as:

- Client's name, unit, or room number
- Admission date, admitting diagnosis
- Proposed length of stay
- Religious affiliation
- Local clergy and telephone number

Assess for potential religious supports:

- Minister, priest, rabbi, shaman, emmen, other
- The need for church or prayer services
- The need for confession, communion, religious music
- The need for a Bible, Koran, Bhagavad-Gita, prayer books

Assess for religious practices:

- Are there special rituals that may need to be honored?
- Are there special health practices that may need to be honored?
- Are there special religious dietary needs?
- Is there a special prayer schedule that should be followed?
- Are there special fasting rituals that should be followed?
- How will the illness affect religious practices?
- How will the illness affect religious rituals?

Assess for religious supports:

- Which religious supports may help your client?
- To whom does the client turn for help?
- How does the client describe his or her family?
- Who is the client's main source of support?
- Who is the client's main source of hope?
- Where does your client turn for comfort?
- What gives your client's life meaning?
- Does your client believe that the illness is a punishment?

PHYSICAL ASSESSMENT

Appearance

Stage of development, general health, striking features, height, weight, behavior, posture, communication skills, grooming, hygiene

Skin

Color, consistency, temperature, turgor, integrity, texture, lesions, mucous membranes

Hair

Color, texture, amount, distribution

Nails

Color, texture, shape, size

Neurologic

Pupil reaction, motor and verbal responses, gait, reflexes, neurologic checks

Musculoskeletal

Range of motion, gait, tone, posture

Cardiovascular

Heart rate and rhythm, Homans' sign, peripheral pulses and temperature, edema

Respiratory

Rate, rhythm, depth, effort, quality, expansion, cough, breath sounds, sputum; production, color, and amount, tracheostomy size, nasal patency

Gastrointestinal
Abdominal contour, bowel sounds, nausea, vomiting, ostomy type and care, fecal frequency, consistency, presence of blood

Genitourinary
Urine color, character, amount, odor, ostomy

Classification of Percussion Sounds			
Sound	**Pitch**	**Duration**	**Example**
Flat	High	Short	Muscle
Dull	Medium	Medium	Liver, heart
Resonant	Low	Long	Lungs
Hyper-resonant	Lower	Longer	Emphysemic lungs
Tympanic	Lowest	Longest	Stomach, colon

ASSESSMENT TECHNIQUES
Inspection By visual or auditory observation
Auscultation By listening to sounds with a stethoscope
Palpation By touching
Fingertips: Best for texture, moisture, shape
Palmar surface of fingers: Best for vibration
Dorsum of hand: Best for temperature
Percussion By striking the body and assessing the sound
Light percussion: Best for tenderness, density
Sharp percussion: Best for reflexes

TEMPERATURE
Normal Oral Averages

	° C	° F
Infant	36-38	97-100
Child	37	98.6
Adult	37	98.6
Elderly	36	98

Time Required for Reading Glass Thermometer

Oral: 3 to 5 minutes
Axillary: 9 to 10 minutes
Rectal: 2 to 4 minutes

Time Required for Reading Electronic Thermometer

Hold the thermometer in place until the light or auditory signal indicates a reading

Time Required for Reading Disposable Thermometer

Hold the thermometer in place until the chemically impregnated dots change color (about 45 seconds)

Time Required for Reading Tympanic Thermometer

Hold the thermometer in place until the reading is displayed (about 2 seconds)

Distance of Insertion for Rectal Thermometer

Child: 1 inch
Adult: 1½ inches

Conversion Used for Fahrenheit

Axillary: Oral minus 1° F
Rectal: Oral plus 1° F

ADVANTAGES AND DISADVANTAGES OF TEMPERATURE MEASUREMENT METHODS

Axilla

Advantages

Safe, inexpensive, and noninvasive

Can be used with newborn or unconscious client

Disadvantages

Takes a long time

Not good for rapid changes

Electronic

Advantages

Rapid measurement, usually 4 seconds

Ideal for children, unbreakable

Disadvantages

May be less accurate

Risk of transferring nosocomials

Mercury

Advantages

Accessible to clients at home

Inexpensive and easy to store

Disadvantages

Risk of breakage

Risk of mercury exposure

Oral

Advantages

Comfortable, accurate, easy to obtain

Reflects rapid change in core temperature

Disadvantages

Not recommended for those who have had oral surgery or who have epilepsy

Rectal

Advantages

Very reliable

Disadvantages

May lag behind core temperature during rapid changes

Should not be used for those with diarrhea or who have had rectal surgery

Skin

Advantages

Safe, inexpensive, and noninvasive

Can be used on neonates

Disadvantages

Lags behind other sites during rapid temperature changes

Tympanic

Advantages

Safe, inexpensive, and noninvasive

Accurate and rapid measurement

Disadvantages

Cannot be used with hearing aides

Otitis media can distort readings

Special Factors
Circadian rhythm Lower temperatures in AM, higher in PM
Hormones Progesterone will raise temperature
Emotions Anxiety will raise temperature

Clinical Signs of Fever
Onset Increased heart rate, increased respirations, pallor, cool skin, cyanosis, chills, decreased sweating, increased temperature
Course Flushed, warm skin, increased heart rate and respiration, increased thirst, mild dehydration, drowsiness, restlessness, decreased appetite, weakness
Abatement Flushed skin, decreased shivering, dehydration, diaphoresis

Fever Patterns
Fungal (infection) Rises slowly and stays high
Intermittent Spikes but falls to normal each day
Persistent Either remains elevated or low grade; often caused by tumors of the central nervous system
Relapsing Febrile for several days, alternating with normal temperatures; often caused by parasites or urinary tract infections
Remittent Spikes and falls, but not to normal; often noted with abscesses, tuberculosis, or influenza viruses
Septic (infection) Wide peak and nadir, often rigors and diaphoresis; often caused by gram-negative organisms
Sustained Same as persistent

THERMAL DISORDERS

Hypothermia Temperature less than 34° C or 94° F
  Treatment: Warm slowly

Frostbite Constriction of vessels, numbness, pale
  skin
  Treatment: Warm slowly

Hyperthermia Any temperature above normal;
  severe hyperthermia is indicated by temperatures
  at or above 42.2° C or 108° F
  Treatment: Replace fluids, watch for chilling

Heatstroke Temperature above 42.2° C or 108° F
  Treatment: Ice to groin and axilla

Heat cramps Spasms of muscles
  Treatment: Replace fluids, watch for chilling

Temperature Conversions		
° F-° C	° F-° C	° F-° C
95.0-35.0	100.2-37.9	105.1-40.6
95.2-35.1	**100.4-38.0**	105.4-40.8
95.4-35.2	100.6-38.1	105.6-40.9
95.5-35.3	100.8-38.2	**105.8-41.0**
95.7-35.4	101.0-38.3	106.0-41.1
95.9-35.5	101.1-38.4	106.2-41.2
96.1-35.6	101.3-38.5	106.3-41.3
96.3-35.7	101.5-38.6	106.5-41.4
96.6-35.9	101.7-38.7	106.7-41.5
96.8-36.0	102.0-38.8	106.9-41.6
97.0-36.1	**102.2-39.0**	107.2-41.8
97.2-36.2	102.4-39.1	107.4-41.9
97.3-36.3	102.6-39.2	**107.6-42.0**
97.5-36.4	102.8-39.3	107.8-42.1
97.7-36.5	103.0-39.4	108.0-42.2
97.9-36.5	103.1-39.5	108.1-42.3
98.2-36.8	103.3-39.6	108.3-42.4
98.4-36.9	103.6-39.8	108.5-42.5
98.6-37.0	103.8-39.9	108.7-42.6
98.8-37.1	**104.0-40.0**	109.0-42.7
99.9-37.2	104.2-40.1	109.2-42.9
99.1-37.3	104.4-40.2	109.4-43.0
99.4-37.3	104.5-40.3	109.6-43.1
99.5-37.5	104.7-40.4	109.8-43.2
100.0-37.8	105.0-40.5	109.9-43.3

To convert to Fahrenheit: F = (C × $\frac{9}{5}$) + 32.
To convert to Celsius: C = (F − 32) × $\frac{5}{9}$.

PULSE
Normal Ranges With Averages
Infant: 90-(160)-160 beats per minute
Child: 80-(100)-120 beats per minute
Adult: Female: 60-(80)-100 beats per minute
       Male: 55-(75)-95 beats per minute

Assessments
Volume/Amplitude of Peripheral Pulses
0 = Absent
1+ = Weak/thready
2+ = Normal
3+ = Bounding

Rhythm
Regular Normal
Regular/irregular Usually regular but occasionally irregular
Bigeminal Skips every other beat (monitor needed for detection)

PULSE POINTS

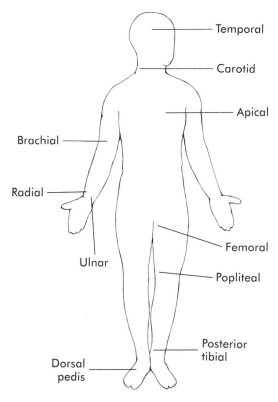

Figure 4-1 Pulse points. (From Potter PA, Perry AG: *Fundamentals of nursing,* ed 5, St Louis, 2001, Mosby.)

RESPIRATION
Normal Ranges
Infant: 30 to 80 respirations per minute
Child: 20 to 30 respirations per minute
Adult: 15 to 20 respirations per minute

Assessments
Depth: Deep or shallow
Rhythm: Even or uneven
Effort: Ease, quiet, or with great effort
Expansion: Symmetric or asymmetric
Cough: Productive, nonproductive, or absent
Auscultation: Clear, good air exchanged throughout;
    adventitious; crackles, wheezes; diminished, low-
    ered, or distant sounds; absent, no sounds

BLOOD PRESSURE
Normal Averages (Systolic/Diastolic)
Newborn: 65-90/30-60 mm Hg
Infant: (1 year) 65-125/40-90 mm Hg
      (2 years) 75-100/40-90 mm Hg
Child: (4 years) 80-120/45-85 mm Hg
      (6 years) 85-115/50-60 mm Hg
Adolescent: (12 years) 95-135/50-70 mm Hg
          (16 years) 100-140/50-70 mm Hg
Adult: (18-60 years) 110-140/60-90 mm Hg
      (60+ years) 120-140/80-90 mm Hg

Orthostatic/Postural Changes
Take blood pressure and pulse with client lying down. Then have client sit or stand for 1 minute. Retake blood pressure and pulse. Record both sets of numbers. If client is orthostatic, pressure will decrease (20-30 mm Hg) and pulse will increase (5-25 beats per minute) when sitting or standing.

Record and report any orthostasis.

Korotkoff Sounds
Sounds of Blood Pressure
Phase I: Systole (sharp thud)
Phase II: Systole (swishing sound)
Phase III: Systole (low thud or knocking)
Phase IV: Diastole (begins fading)
Phase V: Diastole (silence)
Blood volume Amount of blood in the system
Decreased blood volume Equals decreased pressure, meaning increased need for fluids
Increased blood volume Equals increased pressure, meaning need for fewer fluids
Cardiac output Stroke volume multiplied by heart rate

Diastole Ventricular relaxation

Pulse pressure Systole minus diastole (normal range is 25 to 50)

Systole Ventricular contraction

Viscosity Thickness of the blood

Increased viscosity Equals increased pressure, meaning more work on the heart

The Cuff

Cuff should be 20% wider than the diameter of the limb.

Creating a False High Reading
- Having a cuff that is too narrow
- Having a cuff that is too loose
- Deflating the cuff too slowly
- Having the arm below the heart
- Having the arm unsupported

Creating a False Low High Reading
- Having a cuff that is too wide
- Having a cuff that is too tight
- Deflating the cuff too quickly
- Having the arm above the heart

Creating a False Diastolic Reading
- Deflating the cuff too slowly
- Having a stethoscope that fits poorly in the examiner's ears
- Inflating the cuff too slowly

Creating a False Systolic Reading
- Deflating the cuff too quickly

Height and Weight Conversions			
Height			
Inches	**cm**	**cm**	**Inches**
1	2.5	1	0.4
2	5.1	2	0.8
4	10.2	3	1.2
6	15.2	4	1.6
8	20.3	5	2.0
10	25.4	6	2.4
20	50.8	8	3.1
30	76.2	10	3.9
40	101.6	20	7.9
50	127.0	30	11.8
60	152.4	40	15.7
70	177.8	50	19.7
80	203.2	60	23.6
90	227.6	70	27.6
100	254.0	80	31.5
150	381.0	90	35.4
200	508.0	100	39.4

From Thompson JM, Bowers AC: *Clinical outlines for health assessment,* St Louis, 1997, Mosby.
1 inch = 2.54 cm; 1 cm = 0.3937 inch.

Continued

	Height and Weight Conversions—cont'd		
	Weight		
lb	kg	kg	lb
1	0.5	1	2.2
2	0.9	2	4.4
4	1.8	3	6.6
6	2.7	4	8.8
8	3.6	5	11.0
10	4.5	6	13.2
20	9.1	8	17.6
30	13.6	10	22
40	18.2	20	44
50	22.7	30	66
60	27.3	40	88
70	31.8	50	110
80	36.4	60	132
90	40.9	70	154
100	45.4	80	176
150	66.2	90	198
200	90.8	100	220

1 lb = 0.454 kg; 1 kg = 2.204 lb.

1983 Metropolitan Height and Weight Tables for Adults*

MEN			Small Frame			Medium Frame			Large Frame		
Feet	Inches	cm	Pounds	Kilograms†		Pounds	Kilograms†		Pounds	Kilograms†	
5	1	154.9	128-134	58.2-60.9		131-141	59.5-64.1		138-150	62.7-68.2	
5	2	157.5	130-136	59.1-61.8		133-143	60.4-65.0		140-153	63.6-69.5	
5	3	160.0	132-138	60.0-62.7		135-145	61.4-65.9		142-156	64.5-70.9	
5	4	162.6	134-140	60.9-63.6		137-148	62.3-67.2		144-160	65.5-72.7	
5	5	165.1	136-142	61.8-64.5		139-151	63.2-68.6		146-164	66.4-74.5	
5	6	167.6	138-145	62.7-65.9		142-154	64.5-70.0		149-168	67.7-76.4	
5	7	170.2	140-148	63.6-67.2		145-157	65.9-71.4		152-172	69.1-78.2	
5	8	172.7	142-151	64.5-68.6		148-160	67.2-72.7		155-176	70.5-80.0	
5	9	175.3	144-154	65.5-70.0		151-153	68.6-74.1		158-180	71.8-81.8	
5	10	177.8	146-157	66.4-71.4		154-166	70.0-75.5		161-184	73.2-83.6	
5	11	180.3	149-160	67.7-72.7		157-170	71.4-77.3		164-188	74.5-85.5	
6	0	182.9	152-164	69.1-74.5		160-174	72.7-79.1		168-192	76.4-87.3	
6	1	185.4	155-168	70.5-76.4		164-178	74.5-80.9		172-197	78.2-89.5	
6	2	188.0	158-172	71.8-78.2		167-182	75.9-82.7		176-202	80.0-91.8	
6	3	190.5	162-176	73.6-80.0		171-187	77.7-85.0		181-207	82.3-94.1	

Modified from Metropolitan Life Insurance Company. Statistical Bulletin (source of basic data: *1979 Build Study, Society of Actuaries and Association of Life Insurance Medical Directors of America*, 1980). New York, 1983, Metropolitan Life Insurance Company.

Continued

1983 Metropolitan Height and Weight Tables for Adults*—cont'd

WOMEN			Small Frame		Medium Frame		Large Frame	
Feet	Inches	cm	Pounds	Kilograms†	Pounds	Kilograms†	Pounds	Kilograms†
4	9	144.8	102-111	46.4-50.0	109-121	49.5-55.0	118-131	53.6-59.5
4	10	147.3	102-113	46.8-51.4	111-123	50.0-55.9	120-134	54.5-60.9
4	11	149.9	104-115	47.3-52.3	113-126	51.4-57.2	122-137	55.5-62.3
5	0	152.4	106-118	48.2-53.6	115-129	52.3-58.6	125-140	56.8-63.6
5	1	154.9	108-121	49.1-55.0	118-132	53.6-60.0	128-143	58.2-65.0
5	2	157.5	111-124	50.5-56.4	121-135	55.0-61.4	131-147	59.5-66.8
5	3	160.0	114-127	51.8-57.7	124-138	56.4-62.7	134-151	60.9-68.6
5	4	162.6	117-130	53.2-59.0	127-141	57.7-64.1	137-155	62.3-70.5
5	5	165.1	120-133	54.5-60.5	130-144	59.0-65.5	140-159	63.6-72.3
5	6	167.6	123-136	55.9-61.8	133-147	60.5-66.8	143-163	65.0-74.1
5	7	170.2	126-139	57.3-63.2	136-150	61.8-68.2	146-167	66.4-75.9
5	8	172.7	129-142	58.6-64.5	139-153	63.2-69.5	149-170	67.7-77.3
5	9	175.3	132-145	60.0-65.9	142-156	64.6-70.9	152-173	69.1-78.6
5	10	177.8	135-148	61.4-67.3	145-159	65.9-72.3	155-176	70.5-80.0
5	11	180.3	138-151	62.7-73.6	148-162	67.3-73.6	158-179	71.8-81.4

*The weights presented are those associated with the lowest mortality. They are not necessarily the weights at which people are healthiest, perform their jobs optimally, or even look their best. Weights are for persons 25-59 years old (in indoor clothing). Three weight ranges were determined for each sex on each size and attributed to a small, medium, or large frame (in indoor clothing weighing 5 lb for men and 3 lb for women; shoes with 1-inch heels).
†Kilogram ranges determined through direct conversion of pound ranges (# of lb ÷ 2.2 = # of kg).

Chapter 5

Documentation

For an in-depth study of documentation, consult the
following publications:

AJN/Mosby: *Nursing boards review for the NCLEX-RN examination,* ed 10,
    St Louis, 1996, Mosby.
Austrin MG, Austrin HR: *Learning medical terminology,* ed 9, St Louis, 1998,
    Mosby.
Balzer-Riley J: *Communication in nursing: communicating assertively and
    responsibly in nursing,* ed 4, St Louis, 2000, Mosby.
Miller MA: *Critical thinking applied to nursing,* St Louis, 1996, Mosby.
Potter PA, Perry AG: *Fundamentals of nursing,* ed 5, St Louis, 2001, Mosby.

THE NURSING PROCESS

Assessment Data collection; tools used include client and family interviews, functional areas, physical assessments, and laboratory tests; subjective aspects are those observed by client; objective aspects are those observed by nurse

Analysis Interpretation of collected client data: determination of nursing diagnosis and plan of care; formation of nursing diagnoses

Planning Formation of client's plan of care; client goals are outcomes to be achieved by client

Implementation Nursing interventions; client's plan of care is based on assessments, analysis, and expected outcomes

Evaluation Degree to which client's outcomes have been achieved; revision is an alteration in plan of care when expected outcomes are not achieved

EFFECTIVE DOCUMENTATION

Be factual.
Be accurate.
Be complete.
Be concise.
Be current.
Be organized.

NURSING DIAGNOSES BY FUNCTIONAL AREA

Health Perception

Growth and development, delayed
Health maintenance, ineffective
Health-seeking behavior (specify)
Injury, risk for
Injury, perioperative positioning: risk for

Nutrition

Body temperature, imbalanced, risk for
Fluid volume, deficient
Fluid volume, deficient, risk for
Fluid volume excess
Hyperthermia
Hypothermia
Infant feeding pattern, ineffective
Infection, risk for
Nutrition, imbalanced: less than body requirements
Nutrition, imbalanced: more than body requirements
Nutrition, imbalanced: high risk for more than body requirements
Oral mucous membrane, impaired
Swallowing, impaired
Tissue integrity, impaired

Respiration/Circulation

Airway clearance, ineffective
Aspiration, risk for
Breathing pattern, ineffective
Cardiac output, decreased
Gas exchange, impaired
Tissue perfusion, ineffective (specify type) (renal, cerebral, cardiopulmonary, gastrointestinal, peripheral)

Skin integrity, impaired
Skin integrity, impaired: high risk for
Ventilation, impaired spontaneous
Ventilatory weaning process, dysfunctional

Elimination
Bowel incontinence
Constipation
Constipation, perceived
Diarrhea
Incontinence, functional urinary
Incontinence, reflex urinary
Incontinence, stress urinary
Incontinence, total urinary
Incontinence, urge urinary
Urinary elimination, impaired
Urinary retention

Activity/Exercise
Activity intolerance
Activity intolerance, risk for
Disuse syndrome, risk for
Diversional activity, deficient
Energy field, disturbed
Fatigue
Home maintenance, impaired
Mobility, impaired physical
Peripheral neurovascular dysfunction, risk for
Self-care deficit, bathing/hygiene
Self-care deficit, dressing/grooming
Self-care deficit, feeding
Self-care deficit, toileting

Sleep
Sleep pattern, disturbed

Cognition
Confusion, acute
Confusion, chronic
Knowledge, deficient (specify)
Pain, acute
Pain, chronic
Sensory perception, disturbed (specify) (visual, auditory, kinesthetic, gustatory, tactile, olfactory)
Thought process, disturbed

Coping/Stress
Adjustment, impaired
Anxiety
Community coping, readiness for enhanced
Community coping, ineffective
Coping, defensive
Coping, family: readiness for growth
Coping, family: compromised
Coping, family: disabled
Coping, ineffective individual
Denial, ineffective
Fear
Loneliness, risk for
Management of therapeutic regimen, individual ineffective
Management of therapeutic regimen, community ineffective
Management of therapeutic regimen, family ineffective
Poisoning, risk for
Post-trauma syndrome

Rape-trauma syndrome
Rape-trauma syndrome: compound reaction
Rape-trauma syndrome: silent reaction
Relocation stress syndrome
Self-mutilation, risk for
Suffocation, risk for
Violence, risk for: self-directed or other-directed

Self-Perception
Body image, disturbed
Hopelessness
Personal identity, disturbed
Powerlessness
Self-esteem, risk for situational low
Self-esteem, chronic low
Self-esteem, situational low

Role/Relationships
Breastfeeding, effective
Breastfeeding, ineffective
Breastfeeding, interrupted
Caregiver role strain
Caregiver role strain, risk for
Communication, impaired verbal
Environmental interpretation syndrome: impaired
Family processes, dysfunctional: alcoholism
Family processes, interrupted
Grieving, anticipatory
Grieving, dysfunctional
Infant behavior, disorganized
Infant behavior, disorganized: risk for
Infant behavior organized: readiness for enhanced
Noncompliance (specify)
Parenting, impaired
Parenting, impaired, risk for

Parent/infant/child attachment, impaired, risk for
Parental role conflict
Protection, ineffective
Role performance, ineffective
Social interaction, impaired
Social isolation
Trauma, risk for
Unilateral neglect

Sexuality
Sexual dysfunction
Sexuality patterns, ineffective

Values/Beliefs
Spiritual distress (distress of the human spirit)

NANDA NURSING DIAGNOSES TAXONOMY II

Activity intolerance
Risk for Activity intolerance
Impaired Adjustment
Ineffective Airway clearance
Latex Allergy response
Risk for latex Allergy response
Anxiety
Death Anxiety
Risk for Aspiration
Risk for impaired parent/infant/child Attachment
Autonomic dysreflexia
Risk for Autonomic dysreflexia
Disturbed Body image
Risk for imbalanced Body temperature
Bowel incontinence
Effective Breastfeeding
Ineffective Breastfeeding
Interrupted Breastfeeding
Ineffective Breathing pattern
Decreased Cardiac output
Caregiver role strain
Risk for Caregiver role strain
Impaired Comfort
Impaired verbal Communication
Decisional Conflict
Parental role Conflict
Acute Confusion
Chronic Confusion
Constipation
Perceived Constipation
Risk for Constipation
Ineffective Coping
Ineffective community Coping
Readiness for enhanced community Coping

Defensive **C**oping
Compromised family **C**oping
Disabled family **C**oping
Readiness for enhanced family **C**oping
Ineffective **D**enial
Impaired **D**entition
Risk for delayed **D**evelopment
Diarrhea
Risk for **D**isuse syndrome
Deficient **D**iversional activity
Disturbed **E**nergy field
Impaired **E**nvironmental interpretation syndrome
Adult **F**ailure to thrive
Risk for Falls
Dysfunctional **F**amily processes: alcoholism
Interrupted **F**amily processes
Fatigue
Fear
Deficient **F**luid volume
Excess **F**luid volume
Risk for deficient **F**luid volume
Risk for imbalanced **F**luid volume
Impaired **G**as exchange
Grieving
Anticipatory **G**rieving
Dysfunctional **G**rieving
Delayed **G**rowth and development
Risk for disproportionate **G**rowth
Ineffective **H**ealth maintenance
Health-seeking behaviors
Impaired **H**ome maintenance
Hopelessness
Hyperthermia
Hypothermia
Disturbed personal **I**dentity

Functional urinary Incontinence
Reflex urinary Incontinence
Stress urinary Incontinence
Total urinary Incontinence
Urge urinary Incontinence
Risk for urge urinary Incontinence
Disorganized Infant behavior
Risk for disorganized Infant behavior
Readiness for enhanced organized Infant behavior
Ineffective Infant feeding pattern
Risk for Infection
Risk for Injury
Risk for perioperative-positioning Injury
Decreased Intracranial adaptive capacity
Deficient Knowledge
Risk for Loneliness
Impaired Memory
Impaired bed Mobility
Impaired physical Mobility
Impaired wheelchair Mobility
Nausea
Unilateral Neglect
Noncompliance
Imbalanced Nutrition: less than body requirements
Imbalanced Nutrition: more than body requirements
Risk for imbalanced Nutrition: more than body
    requirements
Impaired Oral mucous membrane
Acute Pain
Chronic Pain
Impaired Parenting
Risk for impaired Parenting
Risk for Peripheral neurovascular dysfunction
Risk for Poisoning

Post-trauma syndrome
Risk for Post-trauma syndrome
Powerlessness
Risk for Powerlessness
Ineffective Protection
Rape-trauma syndrome
Rape-trauma syndrome: compound reaction
Rape-trauma syndrome: silent reaction
Relocation stress syndrome
Risk for Relocation stress syndrome
Ineffective Role performance
Bathing/hygiene Self-care deficit
Dressing/grooming Self-care deficit
Feeding Self-care deficit
Toileting Self-care deficit
Chronic low Self-esteem
Situational low Self-esteem
Risk for situational low Self-esteem
Self-mutilation
Risk for Self-mutilation
Disturbed Sensory perception
Sexual dysfunction
Ineffective Sexuality patterns
Impaired Skin integrity
Risk for impaired Skin integrity
Sleep deprivation
Disturbed Sleep pattern
Impaired Social interaction
Social isolation
Chronic Sorrow
Spiritual distress
Risk for Spiritual distress
Readiness for enhanced Spiritual well-being
Risk for Suffocation

Risk for Suicide
Delayed **S**urgical recovery
Impaired **S**wallowing
Effective **T**herapeutic regimen management
Ineffective **T**herapeutic regimen management
Ineffective community **T**herapeutic regimen
    management
Ineffective family **T**herapeutic regimen management
Ineffective **T**hermoregulation
Disturbed **T**hought processes
Impaired **T**issue integrity
Ineffective **T**issue perfusion
Impaired **T**ransfer ability
Risk for **T**rauma
Impaired **U**rinary elimination
Urinary retention
Impaired spontaneous **V**entilation
Dysfunctional **V**entilatory weaning response
Risk for other-directed **V**iolence
Risk for self-directed **V**iolence
Impaired **W**alking
Wandering

Data from North American Nursing Diagnosis Association: *Nursing diagnoses: definitions & classification,* Philadelphia, 2001, The Association.

DEVELOPING A CLIENT'S PLAN OF CARE

The components of the client's plan of care are based on the nursing process, beginning with the client history and assessment. The assessment information is the basis for developing the nursing diagnosis. The client outcomes or intended results are formed to give direction to the nursing interventions. The nursing interventions are the actions needed to achieve the desired client outcomes. The four parts of a care plan are shown on p. 116.

INDIVIDUALIZING CARE PLANS

When a client care plan is developed, the following considerations are needed to individualize the plan to meet each client's needs:

- Age
- Gender
- Level of education
- Developmental level
- General health status (current and before illness)
- Disabilities (physical or mental)
- Strength
- Support systems
- Cultural background
- Spiritual background

Client's Plan of Care

Nursing Diagnosis	Client Outcome	Nursing Intervention	Evaluation
The Nursing Diagnosis List diagnosis	List the goals.	List the interventions	—
Related to Specific problem	Each action should have an outcome.	Actions per nurse	Can the client accomplish goals?
Secondary to Medical diagnosis	Consider the time needed to achieve the goals.	Actions per client	Did the client accomplish goals?
As Manifested by List the signs/symptoms	Consider individualizing the care plan.	Individualize interventions	Did symptoms resolve?

CRITICAL PATHWAYS

Critical pathways, part of managed care, incorporates a multidisciplinary approach to client care. When developing a client's plan of care through the use of critical pathways, consider some of the following questions:

Medicine

Which medical treatments will be recommended for the client? How will the medical treatments affect the plan of care and the client's outcomes? How will the prognosis affect the plan of care and the client's outcomes?

Pharmacy

What medications will be prescribed for the client? How will the medications affect the plan of care and the client's outcomes?

Therapy

Will physical or occupational therapy be prescribed for the client? How will physical or occupational therapy affect the plan of care and the client's outcomes?

What kind of discharge planning will the client need? When in the client's course of treatment should discharge planning begin? How will the discharge plans affect the plan of care and the client's outcomes?

Social Work

Will financial, social, or family services be needed for the client? How will these services affect the plan of care and the client's outcomes?

Chaplain

Will emotional or spiritual support be needed for the client? How will this support affect the plan of care and the client's outcomes?

CHARTING

Source-oriented records Include admission sheet,
  physicians' orders, history, nurses' notes, tests,
  and reports

Problem-oriented records Include database,
  problem list, physicians' orders, care plans, and
  progress notes

Progress Notes

Examples include:

SOAP **S**ubjective data, **O**bjective data, **A**ssessment,
  Plan

SOAPIE **S**ubjective, **O**bjective, **A**ssessment, **P**lan,
  Intervention, **E**valuation

AIR **A**ssessment, **I**ntervention, **R**esults

Narrative Notes written in paragraph form

Flowsheet Notes written in graph or checklist form

The Client's Chart Is a Legal Document

- Be complete, concise, legible, and accurate.
- Use ink, sign all charting, cross out errors with a single line, and initial.
- Do not erase or "white out."
- Do not leave spaces.
- Use only standard nursing abbreviations and proper medical terminology.
- Include date and time.
- Use proper grammar and accurate spelling.
- Documentation can be called as evidence in a legal action.

KARDEX

Includes:

Demographic information

List of medications and IV fluids

List of daily treatments, diagnostic tests, and laboratory tests

Allergies, problem list, activity, diet, and discharge plans

CHANGE-OF-SHIFT REPORT

Includes:

Client's name, age, room number, and diagnosis

Reason for admission, date, and type of surgery, if applicable

Significant changes during the last 24 hours

Tests and procedures during the last shift

Tests and procedures for the upcoming shift

Important laboratory data, current physical and emotional assessments

Vital signs if abnormal, intake and output, IV fluid status

Activity, discharge planning

Updated changes or effectiveness of care plan on appropriate document

Chapter 6

Integumentary System

For an in-depth study of the integumentary system,
consult the following publications:

AJN/Mosby: *Nursing boards review for the NCLEX-RN examination,* ed 10, St Louis, 1993, Mosby.

Austrin MG, Austrin HR: *Learning medical terminology,* ed 9, St Louis, 1998, Mosby.

Barkauskas V, Baumann LC: *Health and physical assessment,* ed 2, St Louis, 1998, Mosby.

Lewis SM, Collier IC, Heitkemper MM: *Medical-surgical nursing,* ed 5, St Louis, 2000, Mosby.

Patton KT, Thibodeau GA: *Handbook for anatomy and physiology,* St Louis, 2000, Mosby.

Potter PA, Perry AG: *Fundamentals of nursing,* ed 5, St Louis, 2001, Mosby.

COMMON INTEGUMENTARY ABNORMALITIES

Type	Characteristics	Assess for
Edema	Fluid accumulation	Trauma, murmur, third heart sound
Diaphoresis	Sweating	Pain, fever, anxiety, insulin reaction
Bromhidrosis	Foul perspiration	Infection, poor hygiene
Hirsutism	Hair growth	Adrenal function
Petechiae	Red/purple spots	Hepatic function, drug reactions
Alopecia	Hair loss	Hypopituitarism, medications, fever, starvation

COMMON SKIN COLOR ABNORMALITIES

Type	Characteristics
Albinism	Decreased pigmentation
Vitiligo	White patches on exposed areas
Mongolian spots	Black and blue spots on back and buttocks
Jaundice	Yellow pigmentation of skin or sclera
Ecchymosis	Black and blue marks; assess for trauma, bleeding time, or hepatic function
Cyanosis	Bluish color of lips, earlobes, or nails; assess lung and heart status

ABNORMALITIES OF THE NAIL BED

160 degrees

180 degrees

180 degrees

Normal nail: Approximately 160-degree angle between nail plate and nail

Clubbing: Change in angle between nail and nail base (eventually larger than 180 degrees); nail bed softening, with nail flattening; often enlargement of fingertips

Causes: Chronic lack of oxygen: heart or pulmonary disease

Beau's lines: Transverse depressions in nails indicating temporary disturbance of nail growth (nail grows out over several months)

Causes: Systemic illness such as severe infection, nail injury

Koilonychia (spoon nail): Concave curves

Causes: Iron deficiency anemia, syphilis, use of strong detergents

Splinter hemorrhages: Red or brown linear streaks in nail bed

Causes: Minor trauma, subacute bacterial endocarditis, trichinosis

Paronychia: Inflammation of skin at base of nail

Causes: Local infection, trauma

Figure 6-1 Abnormalities of nail bed. (From Potter PA, Perry AG: *Fundamentals of nursing,* ed 5, St Louis, 2001, Mosby.)

PRIMARY SKIN LESIONS

Type	Definition	Example
Macule	Flat, nonpalpable	Freckle, measles
Papule	Palpable, <1 cm diameter	Wart, psoriasis
Vesicle	Palpable, <1 cm, with fluid	Blister, chickenpox
Nodule	Hard, <1 cm, into dermis	Dermofibroma
Plaque	Palpable or not, >1 cm	Psoriasis, candidiasis
Bulla	Vesicle, >1 cm	Poison oak, impetigo
Tumor	Nodule, >1 cm	Lipoma, fibroma
Pustule	Pus-filled vesicle	Acne
Wheal	Irregular, flat-topped	—
Cyst	Fluid-filled, large	—

SECONDARY SKIN LESIONS

Type	Definition	Example
Scale	Dead epithelium	Psoriasis
Erosion	Absence of epidermis	Chancre
Crust	Dried exudate	Blister
Fissure	Crack in the epidermis	Cracked lips
Ulcer	Necrotic epidermis	Open sore
Scar	Connective tissue	Healing site
Keloid	Overgrowth of scar	—
Lichenification	Thickening of skin	Eczema
Hyperkeratosis	Thickening of skin	Callus

PRESSURE POINTS

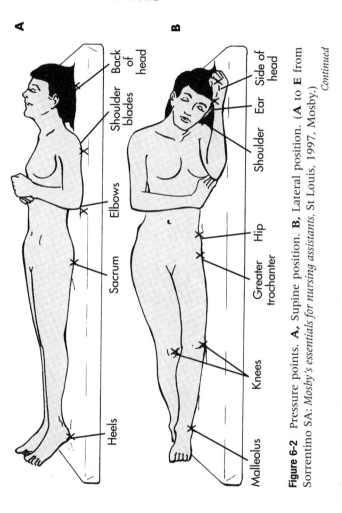

Figure 6-2 Pressure points. **A,** Supine position. **B,** Lateral position. (**A** to **E** from Sorrentino SA: *Mosby's essentials for nursing assistants,* St Louis, 1997, Mosby.)

Continued

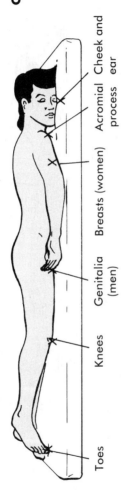

C

Cheek and ear

Acromial process

Breasts (women)

Genitalia (men)

Knees

Toes

Figure 6-2, cont'd   C, Prone position.

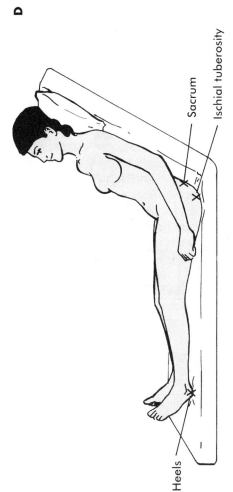

Figure 6-2, cont'd **D,** Fowler's position.

Sacrum

Ischial tuberosity

Heels

Continued

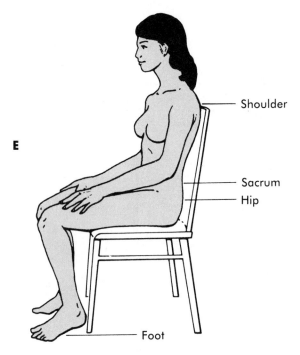

E

Figure 6-2, cont'd   E, Sitting position.

PRESSURE ULCER STAGES

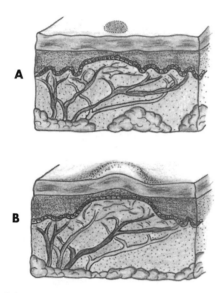

Figure 6-3   Pressure ulcer stages. **A,** Stage I. **B,** Stage II. (Courtesy Laurel Wiersma, RN, MSN, Clinical Nurse Specialist, Barnes Hospital, St Louis, MO. From Potter PA, Perry AG: *Fundamentals of nursing,* ed 5, St Louis, 2001, Mosby.)   *Continued*

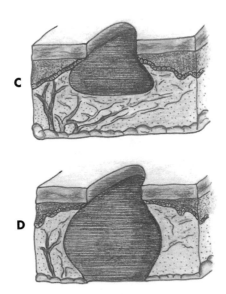

Figure 6-3, cont'd **C,** Stage III. **D,** Stage IV. (Courtesy Laurel Wiersma, RN, MSN, Clinical Nurse Specialist, Barnes Hospital, St Louis, MO. From Potter PA, Perry AG: *Fundamentals of nursing,* ed 5, St Louis, 2001, Mosby.)

The Braden Scale for Predicting Pressure Sore Risk

Patient's Name _____ **Evaluator's Name** _____ **Date of Assessment** _____

Sensory Perception

| Ability to respond meaningfully to pressure-related discomfort | 1. Completely limited: Unresponsive (does not moan, flinch, or grasp) to painful stimuli, due to diminished level of consciousness or sedation. | 2. Very limited: Responds only to painful stimuli. Cannot communicate discomfort except by moaning or restlessness. | 3. Slightly limited: Responds to verbal commands, but cannot always communicate discomfort or need to be turned. | 4. No impairment: Responds to verbal commands. Has no sensory that would limit ability to feel or voice pain or discomfort. |

Copyright Barbara Braden and Nancy Bergstrom, 1986.

Continued

131

Patient's Name _____	Evaluator's Name _____		Date of Assessment _____
	or Limited ability to feel pain over most of body surface.	or Has a sensory impairment which limits the ability to feel pain or discomfort over $\frac{1}{2}$ of body.	or Has some sensory impairment that limits ability to feel pain or discomfort in one or two extremities.	
Moisture Degree to which skin is exposed to moisture	1. Constantly moist: Skin is kept moist almost constantly by perspiration, urine, etc. Dampness is detected every time patient is moved or turned.	2. Very moist: Skin is often, but not always moist. Linen must be changed at least once a shift.	3. Occasionally moist: Skin is occasionally moist, requiring an extra linen change approximately once a day.	4. Rarely moist: Skin is usually dry, linen requires changing only at routine intervals.

Activity

Degree of physical activity

1. Bedfast: Confined to bed.	2. Chairfast: Ability to walk severely limited or nonexistent. Cannot bear own weight and/or must be assisted into chair or wheelchair.	3. Walks occasionally: Walks occasionally during day, but for very short distances, with or without assistance. Spends majority of shift in bed or chair.	4. Walks frequently: Walks outside the room at least twice a day and is outside of room at least once every 2 hours during waking hours.

Mobility

Ability to change and control body position

1. Completely immobile: Does not make even slight changes in body or extremity position without assistance.	2. Very limited: Makes occasional changes but unable to make frequent or significant changes independently.	3. Slightly limited: Makes frequent although slight changes in position independently.	4. No limitations: Makes major and frequent body changes on position independently.

Continued

Copyright Barbara Braden and Nancy Bergstrom, 1986.

The Braden Scale for Predicting Pressure Sore Risk—cont'd

Patient's Name _____ Evaluator's Name _____ Date of Assessment _____

Nutrition

| Usual food intake pattern | 1. Very poor: Never eats a complete meal. Rarely eats more than a third of food offered. Eats two servings or less of protein, meat, or dairy products per day. Takes fluids poorly. Does not take a liquid dietary supplement. or | 2. Probably inadequate: Never eats a complete meal. Rarely eats more than half of food offered. Protein intake includes only three servings of meat or dairy products per day. Occasionally will take a dietary supplement. or | 3. Adequate: Eats over half of meals. Eats a total of four servings of protein each day. Occasionally will refuse a meal but will take a supplement. or Is on tube feeding or TPN regimen that probably meets most of nutritional needs. | 4. Excellent: Eats most of every meal. Usually eats a total of four or more servings of meat and dairy products. Occasionally eats between meals. |

Is NPO and/or maintained on clear liquids or IV lines for more than 5 days.

Receives less than optimum amount of liquid diet or tube feeding.

Friction and Shear

1. Problem: Requires moderate to maximum assistance in moving. Complete lifting without sliding against sheets is impossible. Frequently slides down in bed or chair, requiring frequent repositioning with maximum assistance. Spasticity, contractures, or agitation leads to almost constant friction.

2. Potential problem: Moves feebly or requires minimum assistance. During a move, skin probably slides to some extent against sheets, chair, restraints, or other devices. Maintains relatively good position in chair or bed most of the time but occasionally slides down.

3. No apparent problem: Moves in bed and in chair independently and has sufficient muscle strength to lift up completely during move. Maintains good position in bed or chair at all times.

TOTAL SCORE _____

135

The Mouth

Structure	Normal	Abnormal	Assess for
Lips	Pinkish	Pallor	Anemia
	Bluish (in black clients)	Pallor	Anemia
	Smooth	Blister	Herpes
	Symmetric	Swelling	Allergic reaction
	Moist	Red, cracked	Vitamin B deficiency
Bucca	Pinkish	Pallor	Anemia, leukoplakia/cancer
		Blue	Hypoxia
	Moist	Dry	Dehydration
Gums	Pinkish	Red, swollen	Phenytoin excess, leukemia, vitamin C deficiency
		Dark lines	Bismuth poisoning

Periodontium	Pinkish	Red, swollen	Calcium deposits
Saliva	Moderate	Excessive	9th or 10th cranial nerve injury
Tongue	Centered	Not centered	12th cranial nerve damage
	Dark pink	Red, sore	Anemia
		Decreased papillae	Riboflavin/niacin deficits
	Smooth	Vertical fissure	Dehydration
	Medium sized	Oversized	Hypothyroidism
Uvula	Centered	Not centered	Tumor
	Moves	Does not move	9th or 10th cranial nerve damage
Tonsils	Pink	Red	Pharyngitis
		Swollen	Tonsillitis

Chapter 7

 Skeletal System

For an in-depth study of the skeletal system,
consult the following publications:

AJN/Mosby: *Nursing boards review for the NCLEX-RN examination,* ed 10,
    St Louis, 1996, Mosby.
Austrin MG, Austrin HR: *Learning medical terminology,* ed 9, St Louis, 1998,
    Mosby.
Lewis SM, Collier IC, Heitkemper MM: *Medical-surgical nursing,* ed 5,
    St Louis, 2000, Mosby.
Patton KT, Thibodeau GA: *Handbook for anatomy and physiology,* St Louis,
    2000, Mosby.
Potter PA, Perry AG: *Fundamentals of nursing,* ed 5, St Louis, 2001, Mosby.
Seidel HM, Benedict GW, Ball JW, Dains JE: *Mosby's guide to physical
    examination,* ed 4, St Louis, 1999, Mosby.

SKELETON—ANTERIOR VIEW

1	Cranium	16	Ulna
2	Orbit	17	Radius
3	Maxilla	18	Sacrum
4	Mandible	19	Greater trochanter
5	Clavicle	20	Carpals
6	Sternum	21	Metacarpals
7	Humerus	22	Phalanges
8	Xiphoid process	23	Femur
9	Costal cartilage	24	Patella
10	Vertebral column	25	Tibia
11	Innominate (hip)	26	Fibula
12	Ilium	27	Tarsals
13	Pubis	28	Metatarsals
14	Ischium	29	Phalanges
15	Lesser trochanter		

Figure 7-1 Skeleton—anterior view. (From Austrin MG, Austrin HR: *Learning medical terminology*, ed 9, St Louis, 1998, Mosby.)

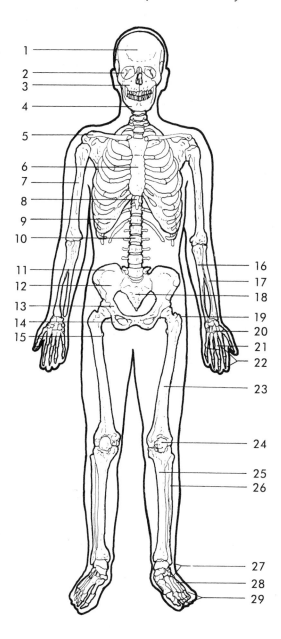

SKELETON—POSTERIOR VIEW

30	Acromion	39	Parietal bone
31	Scapula	40	Occipital bone
32	Humerus	41	Cervical vertebrae (7)
33	Olecranon	42	Thoracic vertebrae (12)
34	Radius	43	Lumbar vertebrae (5)
35	Ulna	44	Ilium
36	Femur	45	Sacrum
37	Fibula	46	Coccyx
38	Tibia	47	Ischium

Figure 7-2 Skeleton—posterior view. (From Austrin MG, Austrin HR: *Learning medical terminology*, ed 9, St Louis, 1998, Mosby.)

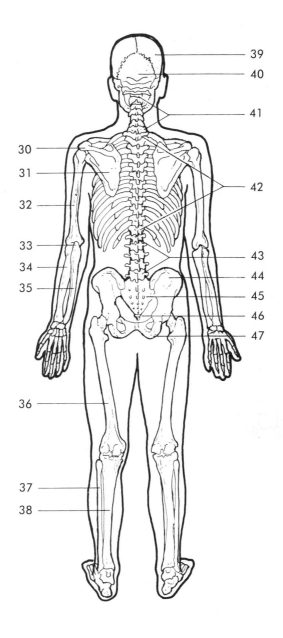

BONES AND SUTURES OF THE SKULL

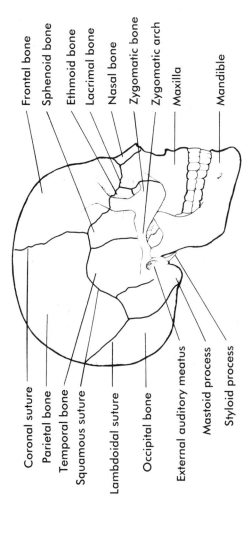

Figure 7-3 Bones and sutures of skull. (From Austrin MG, Austrin HR: *Learning medical terminology*, ed 9, St Louis, 1998, Mosby.)

Frontal bone
Sphenoid bone
Ethmoid bone
Lacrimal bone
Nasal bone
Zygomatic bone
Zygomatic arch
Maxilla
Mandible

Coronal suture
Parietal bone
Temporal bone
Squamous suture
Lambdoidal suture
Occipital bone
External auditory meatus
Mastoid process
Styloid process

TYPES OF FRACTURES

Closed simple Fracture does not break skin

Comminuted Bone is splintered into fragments

Compression Caused by compressive force; common in lumbar vertebrae

Depressed Broken skull bone driven inward

Displaced Fracture produces fragments that become misaligned

Greenstick Fracture where one side of bone is broken and other side is bent

Impacted telescoped Bone is broken and also wedged into another break

Incomplete Continuity of the bone has not been completely destroyed

Longitudinal Break runs parallel with the bone

Oblique Fracture line runs at a 45-degree angle across the longitudinal axis

Open compound Fracture breaks through skin (can be categorized into grades 1 to 4 depending on severity)

Pathologic A disease process weakens bone structure so that a slight degree of trauma can cause fracture (most common in osteoporosis and cancers of the bone)

Segmental Fracture in two places (also called *double fracture*)

Silver-fork Fracture of lower end of radius

Spiral Break coils around the bone; can be caused by a twisting force

Transverse Fracture breaks across the bone at a 90-degree angle along the longitudinal axis

POSSIBLE COMPLICATIONS FROM FRACTURES

Complication	Early Clinical Signs
Pulmonary embolism	Substernal pain, dyspnea, rapid weak pulse; *may occur without symptoms*
Fat embolism	Mental confusion, restlessness, fever, tachycardia, dyspnea
Gas gangrene	Mental aberration, infection
Tetanus	Tonic twitching, difficulty opening mouth; *may occur without symptoms*
Infection	Pain, redness, swelling
Compartment syndrome	Deep localized pain, numbness, weakness
	Decreased circulation distal to the fracture

TYPES OF TRACTION

Traction is a process whereby a steady pull is placed on a part or parts of the body. Traction can be used in reducing a fracture, maintaining a body position, immobilizing a limb, overcoming a muscle spasm, stretching an adhesion, and correcting deformities.

Countertraction A force that pulls against traction

Suspension traction A process to suspend a body part with use of frames, splints, slings, ropes, pulleys, and weights

Skin traction A process of applying wide bands directly to the skin and attaching weights to them (see Buck's and Russell's below)

Buck's traction A process of applying a straight pull on the affected extremity; used for muscle spasms and to immobilize a limb

Russell's traction Knee is suspended in a sling to which a rope is attached; allows for some movement and permits flexion of the knee joint; often used with a femur fracture

Skeletal traction A process whereby traction is applied directly to the bone. A wire or pin is inserted through the bone distal to the fracture

TYPES OF SYNOVIAL JOINTS

Ball and socket Head of one bone fits into socket
of another bone; has greatest range of motion.
Examples: hip and shoulder

Hinge Convex end of one bone fits into concave
end of another bone; movement is on one plane;
joints can flex or extend. *Examples:* elbow, knee,
ankle, fingers, and toes

Pivot Arch shaped; rotates only. *Examples:* C1 and
C2 vertebrae

Saddle Convex bone fits into concave bone; movement is on two planes; joints can flex or extend
and abduct or adduct. *Example:* thumb

Gliding Two flat bones move over each other.
Examples: carpal, tarsal, clavicle, sternum, ribs,
vertebrae, fibula, and tibia

Condyloid Oval; circular movement. *Example:* wrist

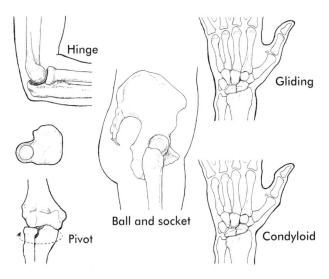

Figure 7-4   Synovial joints. (From Austrin MG, Austrin HR: *Learning medical terminology*, ed 9, St Louis, 1998, Mosby.)

Chapter 8

Muscular System

For an in-depth study of the muscular system,
consult the following publications:

AJN/Mosby: *Nursing boards review for the NCLEX-RN examination,* ed 10,
St Louis, 1996, Mosby.
Austrin MG, Austrin HR: *Learning medical terminology,* ed 9, St Louis, 1998,
Mosby.
Lewis SM, Collier IC, Heitkemper MM: *Medical-surgical nursing,* ed 5,
St Louis, 2000, Mosby.
Patton KT, Thibodeau GA: *Handbook for anatomy and physiology*, St Louis,
2000, Mosby.
Potter PA, Perry AG: *Fundamentals of nursing,* ed 5, St Louis, 2001, Mosby.
Seidel HM, Benedict GW, Ball JW, Dains JE: *Mosby's guide to physical
examination,* ed 4, St Louis, 1999, Mosby.

ANTERIOR SUPERFICIAL MUSCLES

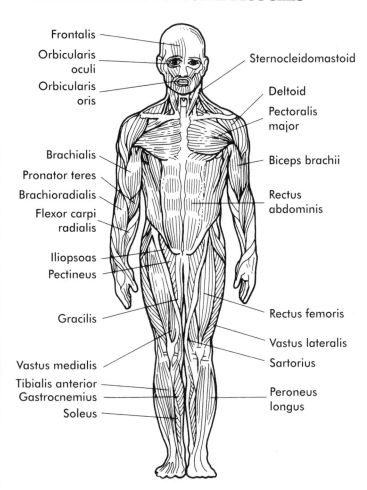

Figure 8-1 Anterior superficial muscles. (From Austrin MG, Austrin HR: *Learning medical terminology*, ed 9, St Louis, 1998, Mosby.)

POSTERIOR SUPERFICIAL MUSCLES

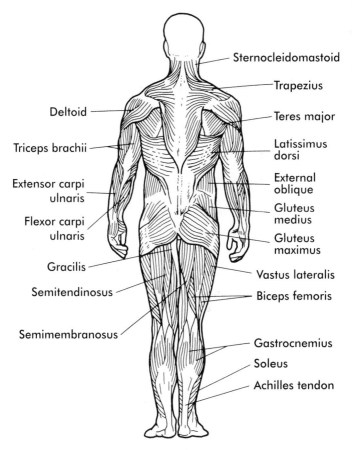

Figure 8-2 Posterior superficial muscles. (From Austrin MG, Austrin HR: *Learning medical terminology*, ed 9, St Louis, 1998, Mosby.)

ANTERIOR FACIAL MUSCLES

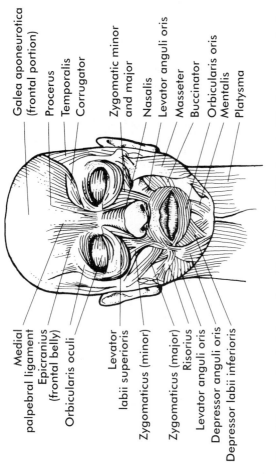

Figure 8-3 Anterior facial muscles. (From Austrin MG, Austrin HR: *Learning medical terminology,* ed 9, St Louis, 1998, Mosby.)

LATERAL FACIAL MUSCLES

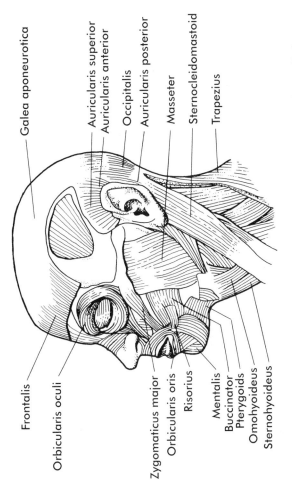

Figure 8-4 Lateral facial muscles. (From Austrin MG, Austrin HR: *Learning medical terminology*, ed 9, St Louis, 1998, Mosby.)

GRADING MUSCLE STRENGTH

Scale	Percent	Interpretation
5	100%	Normal
4	75	Full movement, but not against resistance
3	50	Normal movement against gravity
2	25	Movement if gravity eliminated
1	10	No movement
0	0	Paralysis

EFFECTS OF IMMOBILITY
Benefits
Decreased need for oxygen
Decreased metabolism and energy use
Reduced pain

Bowel Changes
Constipation caused by decreased peristalsis
Poorer sphincter and abdominal muscle tone

Cardiac Changes
Heart rate increase of one-half beat per day, caused by increased sympathetic activity
Decreased stroke volume and cardiac output caused by increased heart rate
Hypotension caused by vasodilatation, leading to thrombosis or edema

Integumentary Changes
Decreased turgor caused by fluid shifts
Increased decubitus ulcers caused by prolonged pressure
Increased skin atrophy caused by decreased nutrition

Metabolic Changes
Decreased metabolic rate
Increased catabolism (protein breakdown) leading to a negative nitrogen imbalance, which results in poorer healing
Hypoproteinemia leading to fluid shifts and edema

Musculoskeletal Changes
Decreased muscle strength of 20% per week
Decreased physical endurance and muscle mass
Muscle atrophy caused by decreased contractions
Osteoporosis caused by increased calcium extraction
Demineralization begins on second day of immobilization

Increased fractures caused by porous bones
Increased hypercalcemia
Muscle shortening leading to contracture

Respiratory Changes
Less alveoli expansion caused by less sighing
Increased mucus in lungs caused by less ability to
    clear them
Decreased chest movement restricts lung expansion
Stiff intercostal muscles caused by less stretching
Shallow respirations leading to decreased capacity
Increased secretions caused by supine position of
    lungs
Less oxygen leading to more carbon dioxide, which
    results in acidosis
Atelectasis caused by decreased blood flow

Neurosensory Changes
Decreased tactile sensation
Increased restlessness, drowsiness, and irritability
Increased confusion and disorientation caused by
    hypercalcemia

Urinary Changes
Poor emptying caused by positioning
Urinary stasis leading to more calcium in kidneys,
    leading to increased renal calculi
Urinary retention and distention caused by poor
    emptying
Incontinence caused by poor muscle tone
Inability to void caused by overstretching of the
    bladder
Infection caused by stasis and alkalinity
Urinary reflux caused by stasis, leading to infections

	Range of Motion (ROM)	
Type	Function	Examples
Flexion	Decrease angle	Bend elbow or knee, chin down, make fist, bend at waist or wrist, lift leg, bend toes
Extension	Increase angle	Straighten elbow or knee, chin straight, hands open, back, fingers, or toes straight
Hyperextension	Straighten joint beyond limits	Head tilted back, fingers pointed up
Abduction	Move away from midline	Legs or arms away from body, fingers spread apart
Adduction	Move toward midline	Legs together, arms at side, fingers together
Rotation	Move around axis	Circle of head, hand, foot, leg, arm, fingers, toes
Eversion	Turn joint outward	Foot or hand pointed away from the body
Inversion	Turn joint inward	Foot or hand pointed toward the body
Pronation	Move joint down	Palm downward, elbow inward
Supination	Move joint up	Palm upward, elbow outward

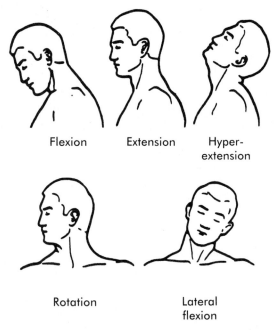

Figure 8-5 Range-of-motion exercises. (From Phipps WJ, Long BC, Woods NF: *Medical-surgical nursing: concepts and clinical practice*, ed 6, St Louis, 1999, Mosby.)

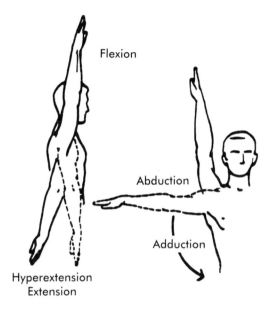

Flexion

Abduction

Adduction

Hyperextension
Extension

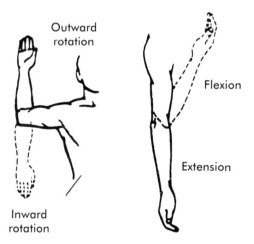

Outward
rotation

Inward
rotation

Flexion

Extension

Figure 8-5, cont'd

Continued

Supination   Pronation

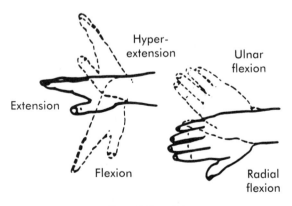

Figure 8-5, cont'd

Abduction   Adduction

Extension   Flexion

Abduction   Opposition   Extension
Adduction   to little   Flexion
             finger

Figure 8-5, cont'd

Continued

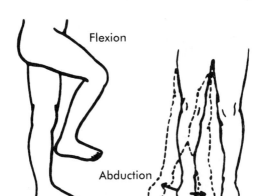

Flexion

Extension

Abduction

Adduction

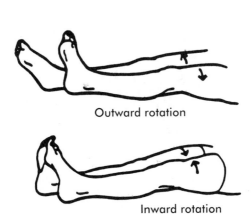

Outward rotation

Inward rotation

Figure 8-5, cont'd

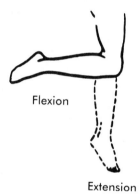

Flexion

Extension

Figure 8-5, cont'd

Continued

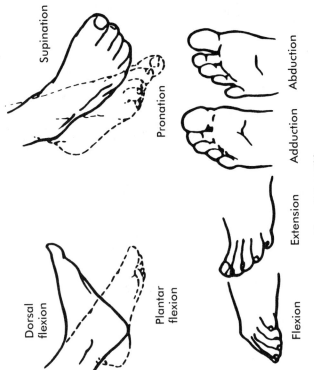

Figure 8-5, cont'd

USE OF HEAT*

Local Effects
Increased skin temperature
Vasodilatation, which increases oxygen and nutrients
    to area
Increased muscle relaxation
Decreased stiffness and spasm
Increased peristalsis

Indications
Stiffness
Arthritis
Pain

Contraindications
Trauma because of increased bleeding
Edema because of increased fluid retention and
    edema
Malignant tumors because of increased cell growth
Burns because of increased cell damage
Open wounds because of increased bleeding
Acute areas such as appendix because of possible
    rupture
Testes because of destruction of sperm
Sensory-impaired clients because of increased chance
    of burns
Confused clients because of increased chance of
    injury

*The use of heat may require a physician's order.

USE OF COLD*
Local Effects
Vasoconstriction, which decreases oxygen to area

Decreased metabolism and thus decreased oxygen needs

Decreased fluid in area and thus decreased swelling

Decreased pain through numbness

Impaired circulation and increased cell death caused by lack of oxygen

Indications
Sprains

Fractures

Swelling

Bleeding

Contraindications
Open wounds, because of decreased chance of healing

Impaired circulation, because of increased chance of injury

Sensory-impaired clients, because of increased chance of injury

Confused clients, because of increased chance of injury

*The use of cold may require a physician's order.

GIVING A MASSAGE

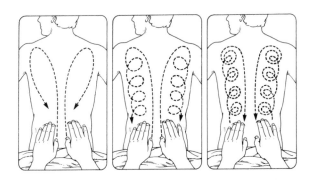

A MASSAGE TECHNIQUE
- Assess if massage is contraindicated.
- Start with the client lying flat or on his or her side.
- Begin with the forehead and work down the body.
- Use a gentle but firm touch.
- Always stroke toward the heart.
- Rub downward on the chest and back.
- Stroke upward on the arms.
- Use a light lotion or oil.

POSITIONING

Dorsal lithotomy Client lies on back with legs well apart. Knees are bent; stirrups are often used. Position is used to examine the bladder, vagina, rectum, or perineum.

Dorsal recumbent Client lies on back with legs slightly apart. Knees are slightly bent, with the soles of the feet flat on the bed.

Fowler's Client is partly sitting with knees slightly bent. The head of the bed can be at semi-Fowler's (45 degrees) or high Fowler's (90 degrees).

Knee-chest Client rests on knees and chest, with head turned to the side. Position is used to examine the rectum or vagina.

Left lateral Client lies on left side, hips closer to the edge of the bed.

Left Sims' Client lies on left side, with right knee bent against the abdomen. Used in rectal examinations and giving enemas.

Prone Client lies on abdomen with arms at sides.

Reverse Trendelenburg Client lies on back with legs together. Bed is straight, with head of bed higher than the foot.

Side lying Client head is in straight line with spine. Use pillows to support head, arms, and upper leg.

Supine (horizontal recumbent) Client lies on back with legs together and extended.

Trendelenburg Client lies on back with legs together. Bed is straight, with head of bed lower than the foot. Used in pelvic surgery.

Positions for Examination

Position	Areas Assessed	Rationale	Limitations
Sitting	Head and neck, back, posterior thorax and lungs, anterior thorax and lungs, breasts, axillae, heart, vital signs, and upper extremities	Sitting upright provides full expansion of lungs and provides better visualization of symmetry of upper body parts.	Physically weakened client may be unable to sit. Examiner should use supine position with head of bed elevated instead.

From Potter PA, Perry AG: *Fundamentals of nursing*, ed 5, St Louis, 2001, Mosby.

Continued

	Positions for Examination—cont'd		
Position	Areas Assessed	Rationale	Limitations
Supine	Head and neck, anterior thorax and lungs, breasts, axillae, heart, abdomen, extremities, pulses	This is most normally relaxed position. It prevents contracture of abdominal muscles and provides easy access to pulse sites.	If client becomes short of breath easily, examiner may need to raise head of bed.
Dorsal recumbent	Head and neck, anterior thorax and lungs, breasts, axillae, heart	Clients with painful disorders are more comfortable with knees flexed.	Position is not used for abdominal assessment because it promotes contracture of abdominal muscles.

| Lithotomy | Female genitalia and genital tract | This position provides maximal exposure of genitalia and facilitates insertion of vaginal speculum. | Lithotomy position is embarrassing and uncomfortable, so examiner minimizes time that client spends in it. Client is kept well draped. Client with severe arthritis or other joint deformity may be unable to assume this position. |
| Sims' | Rectum and vagina | Flexion of hip and knee improves exposure of rectal area. | Joint deformities may hinder client's ability to bend hip and knee. |

Continued

From Potter PA, Perry AG: *Fundamentals of nursing*, ed 5, St Louis, 2001, Mosby.

Positions for Examination—cont'd

Position	Areas Assessed	Rationale	Limitations
Prone	Musculoskeletal system	This position is used only to assess extension of hip joint.	This position is intolerable for client with respiratory difficulties.
Knee-chest	Rectum	This position provides maximal exposure of rectal area.	This position is embarrassing and uncomfortable. Clients with arthritis or other joint deformities may be unable to assume this position.

From Potter PA, Perry AG: *Fundamentals of nursing*, ed 5, St Louis, 2001, Mosby.

Chapter 9

 Nervous System

For an in-depth study of the nervous system,
consult the following publications:

Lewis SM, Collier IC, Heitkemper MM: *Medical-surgical nursing,* ed 5,
    St Louis, 2000, Mosby.
Potter PA, Perry AG: *Fundamentals of nursing,* ed 5, St Louis 2001, Mosby.

STRUCTURES OF THE BRAIN

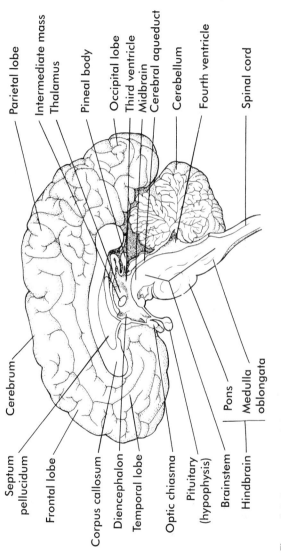

Figure 9-1 Structures of the brain. (From Austrin MG, Austrin HR: *Learning medical terminology*, ed 9, St Louis, 1998, Mosby.)

LEVELS OF CONSCIOUSNESS

Alert Awake and aware, responds appropriately, begins conversation (A&O × 3; alert and oriented to person, place, time)

Lethargic Sleeps but easily aroused, speaks and responds slowly but appropriately

Obtunded Difficult to arouse, slow to respond, and returns to sleep quickly

Stuporous Aroused only through pain; no verbal response, never fully awake

Semicomatose Responds only to pain but has gag and blink reflexes

Comatose No response to pain; no reflexes or muscle tone

NEUROLOGIC FUNCTION

Cerebral

Includes mental status, thought processes, emotions, level of consciousness, orientation, memory, language, appropriateness, intelligence, and developmental age

Cranial Nerves

For a summary of the cranial nerves, see p. 187

Cerebellar

Includes coordination and balance; muscle size, strength, and tone (see p. 156); and evaluation of reflexes

Glasgow Coma Scale		
		Response
Best Eye Opening Response	Spontaneously	4
	To speech	3
(Record "C" if eyes closed by swelling)	To pain	2
	No response	1
Best Motor Response to Painful Stimuli	Obeys verbal command	6
	Localizes pain	5
(Record best upper limb response)	Flexion-withdrawal	4
	Flexion-abnormal	3
	Extension-abnormal	2
	No response	1
Best Verbal Response	Oriented × 3	5
(Record "E" if endotracheal tube in place; "T" if tracheostomy tube in place)	Conversation confused	4
	Speech inappropriate	3
	Sounds incomprehensible	2
	No response	1

Modified from Thompson JM et al: *Mosby's clinical nursing*, ed 4, St Louis, 1997, Mosby.

WARNING SIGNS OF IMPENDING STROKE
- Numbness of face, arm, or leg
- Weakness of face, arm, or leg
- Difficulty speaking or understanding
- Sudden decreased or blurred vision
- Loss of balance
- Dizziness when accompanied by any of the above signs

Neurologic Deficits by Location

Location	Possible Deficits	Management
Frontal lobe	Weakness with plegia Expressive aphasia Focal or grand mal seizures Impaired thought, reasoning and memory, emotional or personality changes	Assess function, PT/OT Assess for speech therapy Educate family on seizures Coordinate neuropsychologic evaluation
Temporal lobe	Visual field loss, impaired memory Temporal lobe seizures Receptive aphasia, dysnomia	Assess visual problems Monitor for seizures Assess speech impairment
Parietal lobe	Sensory deficits, impaired joint position, vibration, light touch	Assess level of neglect Refer to PT/OT for assistance

	Impaired left-right discrimination	Educate family regarding deficits
	Sensory seizures, visual field loss	Monitor for seizures
Occipital lobe	Visual hallucinations	Refer to ophthamologist if needed
	Seizures	Monitor for seizures
		Educate and support family
Cerebellum	Decreased coordination, ataxia	Assess level of deficit
	Nystagmus, increased headaches	Educate and support client
	Increased intracranial pressure	Monitor headaches
Brainstem	Cranial nerve palsies, ataxia	Assess level of deficit
	Sensory or motor impairment	Safety precautions
	Sudden death	Educate and support family

PT, Physical therapy; *OT,* occupational therapy.

CARE OF THE CLIENT WITH SEIZURES
Equipment and Procedures

Bed should be in the lowest position.

Side rails should be in the upright position and padded.

Oxygen and suction equipment should be in room, with IV access.

Indicate "seizure precautions" on critical pathway or plan of care.

Note if client has an aura before seizures.

Use digital thermometers, NOT glass thermometers.

Clients should shower rather than use a tub.

Do not allow the client to leave the unit alone.

Always transport the client with portable oxygen.

Clients with frequent generalized atonic seizures should wear a helmet.

During the Seizure

Call for help, but DO NOT try to restrain the person.

Help the person to lie down and place something soft under the head.

Turn the person on his or her side if possible.

Remove glasses and loosen tight clothing.

DO NOT attempt to place anything between the teeth.

DO NOT attempt to remove dentures.

Monitor the duration of the seizure and the type of movement.

STAY WITH THE PERSON UNTIL THE PERSON IS FULLY ALERT.

After the Seizure

Turn the person to one side to allow saliva to drain; suction if needed.

Perform vital signs and neurologic checks as needed.

DO NOT offer food or drink until the person is fully awake.

Reorient the person, and then allow him or her to rest.

Notify physician *unless* person is being monitored specifically for seizures.

Notify physician *immediately* if seizure occurs without regaining consciousness.

Notify physician *immediately* if an injury occurred during the seizure.

Record all observations made during and immediately after the seizure.

Document the time and length of the seizure and if there was an aura.

Document the sequence of behaviors during the seizures (eye movement, and so on).

Document an injury and what was done about it.

Note what happened with the person just after the seizure (did he or she reorient?).

A CLIENT'S SLEEP HISTORY

- Have the client describe his or her specific problem.
- Have the client describe his or her symptoms and alleviating factors.
- Assess the client's normal sleep pattern.
- Assess the client's normal bedtime rituals.
- Assess for current or recent physical illnesses.
- Assess for current or recent emotional stress.
- Assess for possible sleep disorders.
- Assess the client's current medications and their possible effects on sleep.

SLEEP DISORDERS

Bruxism Tooth grinding during sleep

Insomnia Chronic difficulty with sleep patterns

   Initial insomnia Difficulty falling asleep

   Intermittent insomnia Difficulty remaining asleep

   Terminal insomnia Difficulty going back to sleep

Narcolepsy Difficulty in regulating between sleep and awake states; person may fall asleep without warning

Nocturnal enuresis Bedwetting

Sleep apnea Intermittent periods of cessation of breathing during sleep

Sleep deprivation Decrease in the amount and quality of sleep

Somnambulism Sleepwalking, night terrors, or nightmares

Drugs and Their Effects on Sleep

Hypnotics
- Interfere with reaching deeper sleep stages
- Provide only temporary (1-week) increase in quantity of sleep
- Eventually cause "hangover" during day: excess drowsiness, confusion, decreased energy
- May worsen sleep apnea in older adults

Diuretics
- Cause nocturia

Antidepressants and Stimulants
- Suppress rapid eye movement (REM) sleep

Alcohol
- Speeds onset of sleep
- Disrupts REM sleep
- Awakens person during night and causes difficulty returning to sleep

Caffeine
- Prevents person from falling asleep
- May cause person to awaken during night

From Potter PA, Perry AG: *Fundamentals of nursing,* ed 5, St Louis, 2001, Mosby. *Continued*

Drugs and Their Effects on Sleep—cont'd

Digoxin
- Causes nightmares

Beta-Blockers
- Cause nightmares
- Cause insomnia
- Cause awakening from sleep

Valium
- Decreases stages 2 and 4 and REM sleep
- Decreases awakenings

Narcotics (Morphine/Meperidine [Demerol])
- Suppress REM sleep
- If discontinued quickly, can increase risk of cardiac dysrhythmias because of "rebound REM" periods
- Cause increased awakenings and drowsiness

SEDATION SCALE
S = Sleepy, but easy to arouse
1 = Awake and alert
2 = Slightly drowsy, but easy to arouse
3 = Drowsy, drifts to sleep during conversation
4 = Somnolent, minimal or no response to physical stimulation

Modified from McCaffery M, Pasero C: *Pain: clinical manual*, p. 267, St Louis, 1999, Mosby.

PERIPHERAL NERVES

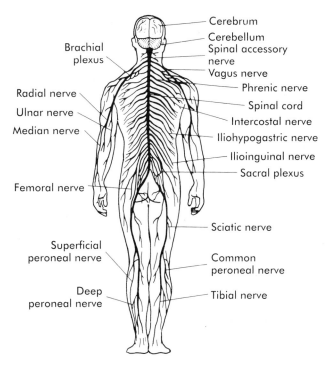

Figure 9-2 Peripheral nervous system, with some cranial nerves.

Assessing Motor Function

Level of Spinal Cord	Assessment: Note Response to the Items Below
C4 to C5	Have the client shrug his or her shoulders against your hands, or apply resistance by pushing downward on the client's shoulders.
C5 to C6	Have the client flex his or her arm at the elbow while you apply resistance by pushing the arm away from the client.
C7	Have the client straighten his or her flexed arm and try to keep it flexed while you apply resistance.
	Have the client pinch his or her thumb and index finger together and hold firmly while you try to pull them apart.
C8 to T1	Have the client squeeze your fingers.
L2 to L4	Have the client lift his or her leg from a lying position while you apply resistance by pushing the leg down.
	Have the client extend his or her leg from the knee-flexed position while you apply resistance to keep the knee flexed.
L5	Have the client dorsiflex his or her feet upward while you apply resistance to the dorsal aspects of the feet.
L5 to S1	Have the client bend at the knee while you apply resistance against the move.
S1	Have the client plantar flex the feet downward while you apply resistance to the plantar aspects of the feet.

	Cranial Nerves			
Number	Name	Type	Function	Method of Assessment
I	Olfactory	Sensory	Smell	Identify odors
II	Optic	Sensory	Vision	Snellen chart
III	Oculomotor	Motor	Vision	Pupil reaction
IV	Trochlear	Motor	Vision	Vertical vision
		Sensory	Cornea	Blink reflex
V	Trigeminal	Motor	Chewing	Clench teeth
VI	Abducens	Motor	Vision	Lateral vision
VII	Facial	Sensory	Taste	Identify tastes
		Motor	Expression	Smile/frown
VIII	Acoustic	Sensory	Equilibrium	Weber's and Rinne tests
IX	Glossopharyngeal	Sensory	Taste	Identify tastes
		Motor	Swallows	Gag reflex
X	Vagus	Sensory	Pharynx	Identify tastes
		Motor	Vocal	Voice tones
XI	Accessory	Motor	Shoulders	Shrug shoulders
XII	Hypoglossal	Motor	Tongue	Protruding tongue

Types of Reflexes		
Name	**Elicited by**	**Response**
Babinski	Stroking lateral sole of foot	Great toe fans out
Chaddock	Stroking below lateral malleolus	Great toe fans out
Oppenheim	Stroking tibial surface	Great toe fans out
Gordon	Squeezing calf muscle	Great toe fans out
Hoffmann	Flicking middle finger down	Flexion of the thumb
Ankle clonus	Brisk dorsiflexion of foot with knee flexed	Up and down movement of the foot
Kernig	Straightening leg with thigh muscle flexed	Pain along posterior of thigh
Brudzinski	Flexing chin on chest	Limitations with pain

REFLEX GRADING SCALE

Grade	Symbol	Interpretation
5	5+	Hyperactive (with clonus)
4	4+	Hyperactive (very brisk)
3	3+	Brisk
2	2+	Normal (average)
1	1+	Diminished but present
0	0	Absent

PAIN ASSESSMENT

Gather information about the client's condition in the following areas:

Definition

The words used by the client to describe pain, such as pressure, stabbing, sharp, tingling, dull, heavy, or cold. *It is important to use and understand the client's language concerning pain and to believe the client who reports pain.*

Onset

When did the pain first begin (date and time)?

Duration

How long does the pain last (persistent, minutes to hours, comes and goes, seconds)? Does the pain occur at the same time each day?

Location

In what area of the body does the pain begin? It may be helpful to have the client point to the exact area if possible. NOTE: A client may say the pain is in the stomach but may point over the lower abdominal area. Also ask if the pain radiates, moves, or goes to a different area of the body. Have the client point to these areas as well.

Severity

How bad is the pain? Or have the client rate the pain. Have a rating scale ready to use and explain your scale. Use the same scale in subsequent assessments. *Examples:* A 0 to 10 scale with 0 being no pain and 10 being the worst pain, or a color scale with blue being no pain and red being the worst pain.

Precipitating Factors
What was the client doing before the pain began (exercise, bending over, work)?

Aggravating Factors
What makes the pain worse?

Alleviating Factors
What makes the pain get better or go away (pain medications, relaxation, rest, music)?

Associated Factors
Nausea or vomiting?
Anger or agitation?
Depression or drowsiness?
Fatigue or sleeplessness?

Observed Behaviors
Agitation or restlessness?
Bracing or fidgeting?
Rubbing or guarding?
Not eating or sleeping?

Vocalizations
Crying or moaning?
Gasping or groaning?
Sighing or noisy breathing?

Facial Expressions
Grimacing or clenched teeth?
Wincing or furrowed brow?
Sadness or eyes closed?
Frightened or tightened lips?

PAIN RATING SCALES

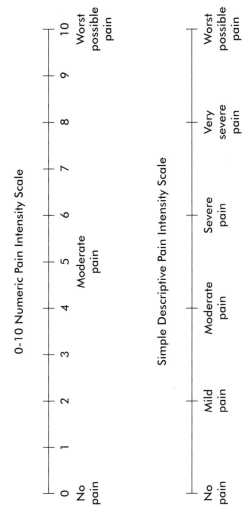

0-10 Numeric Pain Intensity Scale

Simple Descriptive Pain Intensity Scale

Figure 9-3 Pain rating scales. (From Austrin MG, Austrin HR: *Learning medical terminology*, ed 9, St Louis, 1998, Mosby.)

NONPHARMACOLOGIC TREATMENTS OF PAIN

Biofeedback Clients can learn to control muscle tension to reduce pain with the use of biofeedback units.

Cold Used to decrease pain or swelling (See p. 168.)

Distraction Turning the client's attention to something other than the pain, such as music, visitors, or scenery

Heat Used to decrease tension (See p. 167.)

Imagery Uses the client's imagination to create pleasant mental pictures. These pictures are a form of distraction. This activity is said to be a form of self-hypnosis.

Massage (See p. 169.)

Menthol Used to increase blood circulation to painful areas

Nerve blocks Used to block severe, unrelieved pain. A local anesthetic, sometimes combined with cortisone, is injected into or around a nerve.

Positioning (See p. 170.)

Pressure Used to stimulate blood flow to painful areas. Apply firm but not excess pressure for 10 to 60 seconds.

Range of motion exercises (See p. 159.)

Relaxation Relieves pain by reducing muscle tension. Music or relaxation tapes may be helpful.

TENS (transcutaneous electric nerve stimulation) A mild electric current is thought to interrupt pain impulses.

Vibration Used to stimulate blood flow to painful areas

CHRONIC NONMALIGNANT PAIN: NURSING CARE GUIDELINES*

Do not argue with the client about whether the client is in pain.

Do not refer to the client as a narcotics addict.

Do not tell the client that he or she will become an addict if he or she continues to receive narcotics.

Do not use a placebo to try to determine if the client has "real" pain.

Be alert to any changes in the client's pain condition or pain regimen.

Recognize the differences between acute and chronic pain.

Avoid sudden withdrawal of narcotics or sedatives from a client with chronic pain.

When analgesics are required, give them orally if possible. (The effects of oral analgesics will generally last longer than IV or IM medications.)

Review analgesics being used for relief of chronic versus acute pain.

Offer pain relief alternatives. (See p. 194.)

Review the client's support systems and suggest additional ones if appropriate.

Help those living with the client to understand the client's pain management routine.

Assess the client for depression, anxiety, and stress. (Additional stresses may add to the client's overall pain experience.)

Assess suicidal risk.

*Modified from McCaffery M, Beebe A: *Pain: clinical manual for nursing practice,* St Louis, 1989, Mosby.

Average Adult Doses for Analgesics				
Drug	IM Dose (mg/ml)	Oral Dose (mg)*	Half-Life (hr)	Duration (hr)
Aspirin	—	500-1000	15-30 min	4-6
Acetaminophen	—	500-1000	2-3	4-6
Ibuprofen	—	400-800	1.8-2.5	4-6
Salicylate (e.g., Trilisate)	—	500-1000	1-4	6-12
Naproxen	—	500	2-3	6-8
Indomethacin	—	25-75	4-6	8-12
Ketorolac	30-60	10-20	2-3	6
	15-30	—	2-3	6

Oxycodone with acetaminophen (Percocet)	—	5	2-3	4-6
Propoxyphene (Darvon)	—	32-65	1-2	4-6
Levorphanol	2	2-4	2-4	4-8
Morphine	2-15	10-60	1-3	3-7
Codeine	30-60	15-60	2-4	4-6
Hydromorphone (Dilaudid)	1-4	1-10	2-3	4-5
Meperidine (Demerol)	50-100	50-150	1-2	2-4
Methadone	2.5-10	5-40	1-3	4-6
Tramadol (Ultram)	—	50-100	6-8	3-7

Data from *Drug Facts & Comparisons*, St. Louis, 2002, Facts & Comparisons; *Physician's desk reference*, ed 54, Montvale, NJ, 2000, Medical Economics.

* Oral dose=usual dosage range for single dose.

THE EYE

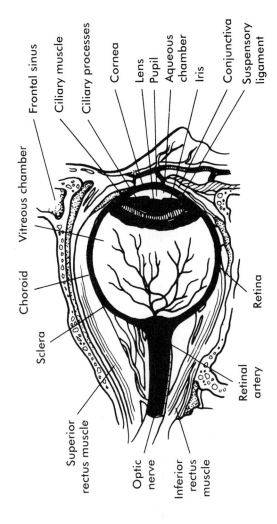

Figure 9-4 Structures of the eye. (From Austrin MG, Austrin HR: *Learning medical terminology,* ed 9, St Louis, 1998, Mosby.)

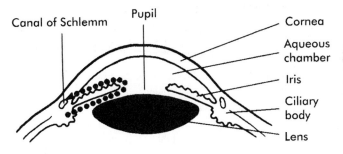

Figure 9-4, cont'd

PUPIL SIZE

Figure 9-5 Chart showing pupil sizes in millimeters. (From Elkin MK, Perry AG, Potter PA: *Nursing interventions and clinical skills*, St Louis, 1996, Mosby.)

Contact Lens Care

Do

- Wash and rinse hands thoroughly before handling a lens.
- Keep fingernails clean and short.
- Remove lenses from their storage case one at a time and place on the eye.
- Start with the same lens (left or right) each time of insertion.
- Use lens placement technique learned from eye specialist.
- Use proper lens care products.
- Wear lenses daily and follow the prescribed wearing schedule.
- Remove a lens if it becomes uncomfortable.
- Keep regular appointments with the eye specialist.
- Remove lenses during sunbathing, showering, or swimming.

Do Not

- Use soaps that contain cream or perfume for cleaning lenses
- Let fingernails touch lenses
- Mix up lenses
- Exceed prescribed wearing time
- Use saliva to wet lenses
- Use homemade saline solution or tap water to wet or clean lenses
- Borrow or mix lens care solution

From Potter PA, Perry AG: *Fundamentals of nursing*, ed 5, St Louis, 2001, Mosby.

BRAILLE ALPHABET

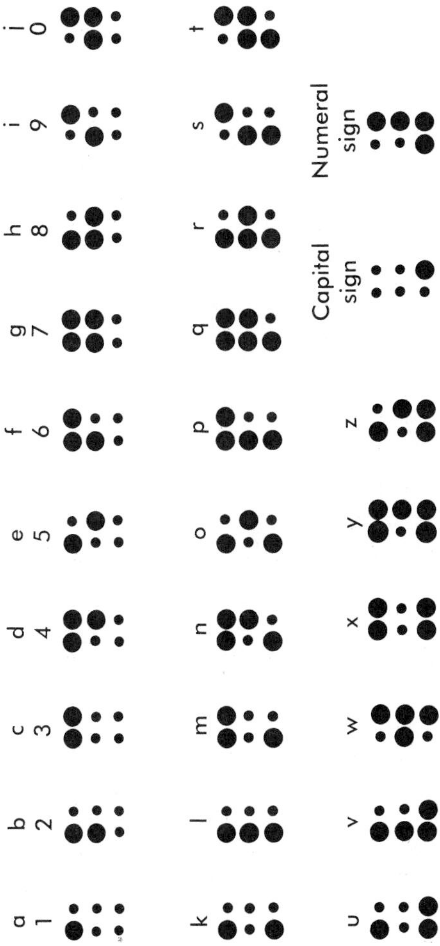

Figure 9-6 Braille alphabet. (From Sorrentino SA: *Mosby's textbook for nursing assistants,* ed 3, St Louis, 1992, Mosby.)

THE EAR

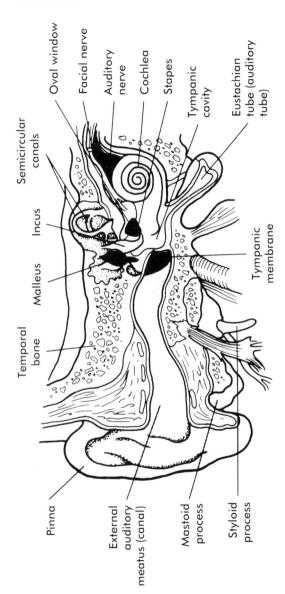

Figure 9-7 Structures of the ear. (From Austrin MG, Austrin HR: *Learning medical terminology*, ed 9, St Louis, 1998, Mosby.)

Assessing Client's Use of Sensory Aids

Eyeglasses
- Purpose for wearing glasses (e.g., reading, distance, or both)
- Methods used to clean glasses
- Presence of symptoms (e.g., blurred vision, photophobia, headaches, irritation)

Contact Lenses
- Type of lens worn
- Frequency and duration of time lenses are worn (including sleep time)
- Presence of symptoms (e.g., burning, excess tearing, redness, irritation, swelling, sensitivity to light)
- Techniques used by the client to clean, store, insert, and remove lenses
- Use of eyedrops or ointments
- Use of emergency identification bracelet or card that warns others to remove client's lenses in case of emergency

Artificial Eye
- Method used to insert and remove eye
- Method for cleaning eye
- Presence of symptoms (e.g., drainage, inflammation, pain involving the orbit)

Hearing Aid
- Type of aid worn
- Methods used to clean aid
- Client's ability to change battery and adjust hearing-aid volume

---

From Potter PA, Perry AG: *Fundamentals of nursing,* ed 5, St Louis, 2001, Mosby.

SIGN LANGUAGE

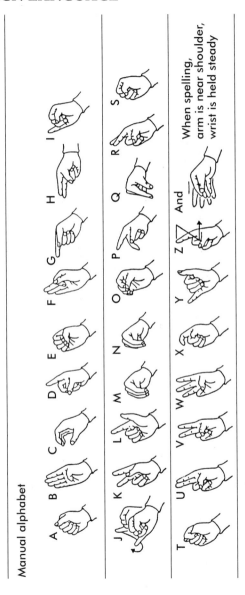

Figure 9-8 Sign language alphabet.

Numbers

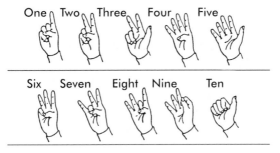

Figure 9-8, cont'd Sign language numbers.

TIPS FOR COMMUNICATING WITH OLDER ADULTS

- First, get the person's attention. This will help if the person is hard of hearing.
- Sit face to face. Lip reading may be helpful.
- Appropriate lighting is important. Avoid glare and dimly lit areas.
- Maintain good eye contact. This will help to instill trust.
- Speak slowly and clearly. This will help if the person is hard of hearing.
- Use short simple words and phases.
- Ask one question at a time. This may help with sensory overload.
- Give the person extra time to answer. This will help if the person is hard of hearing.
- Repeat statements or ideas if needed.
- Rephrase, if needed, but do not change the meaning from the first statement.
- Minimize visual and auditory distractions.
- Do not shout. Remember, not everyone is deaf.
- Summarize points if you are not being understood.
- Expect errors or emotional outbursts in a confused person.
- You may need to start the conversation all over.
- You may need to stop the conversation if the person is unable to communicate.

Chapter 10

Circulatory System

For an in-depth study of the circulatory system,
consult the following publications:

Austrin MG, Austrin HR: *Learning medical terminology,* ed 9, St Louis, 1998,
    Mosby.
Guzzetta CE, Dossey BM: *Cardiovascular nursing: holistic practice,* St Louis,
    1992, Mosby.
Lewis SM, Collier IC, Heitkemper MM: *Medical-surgical nursing,* ed 5,
    St Louis, 2000, Mosby.
Potter PA, Perry AG: *Fundamentals of nursing,* ed 5, St Louis, 2001, Mosby.

PRINCIPAL ARTERIES OF THE BODY

1 Angular
2 Right common carotid
3 Brachiocephalic
4 Arch of aorta
5 Right coronary
6 Left coronary
7 Aorta
8 Celiac
9 Superior mesenteric
10 Common iliac
11 Internal iliac (hypogastric)
12 External iliac
13 Deep medial circumflex femoral
14 Deep femoral
15 Femoral
16 Popliteal
17 Anterior tibial
18 Peroneal
19 Posterior tibial
20 Dorsal pedis
21 Arcuate
22 Dorsal metatarsal
23 Occipital
24 Internal carotid
25 External carotid
26 Left common carotid
27 Subclavian
28 Pulmonary
29 Lateral thoracic
30 Axillary
31 Brachial
32 Splenic
33 Renal
34 Inferior mesenteric
35 Radial
36 Ulnar
37 Deep palmar arch
38 Superficial palmar arch
39 Digital

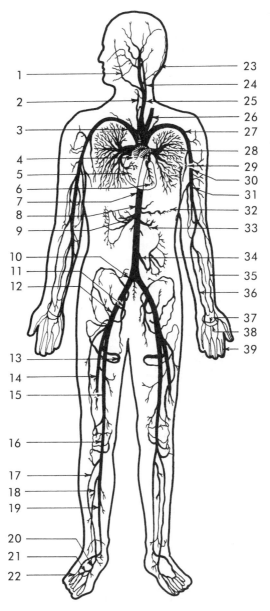

1

2

3

4
5
6
7
8
9

10
11
12

13

14
15

16

17
18
19

20
21
22

23
24
25
26
27

28

29
30
31
32
33

34

35
36

37
38
39

Figure 10-1 Principal arteries of the body. (From Austrin MG, Austrin HR: *Learning medical terminology,* ed 9, St Louis, 1998, Mosby.)

PRINCIPAL VEINS OF THE BODY

1 Angular
2 Anterior facial
3 Internal jugular
4 Right brachiocephalic
5 Subclavian
6 Superior vena cava
7 Right pulmonary
8 Right coronary
9 Inferior vena cava
10 Hepatic
11 Portal
12 Superior mesenteric
13 Common iliac
14 Superior sagittal sinus
15 Inferior sagittal sinus
16 Straight sinus
17 Transverse sinus
18 Cervical plexus
19 External jugular
20 Left brachiocephalic
21 Left pulmonary
22 Cephalic
23 Axillary
24 Left coronary
25 Basilic
26 Splenic
27 Median basilic
28 Long thoracic
29 Inferior mesenteric
30 Internal iliac (hypogastric)
31 External iliac
32 Volar digital
33 Femoral
34 Great saphenous
35 Popliteal
36 Peroneal
37 Posterior tibial
38 Anterior tibial
39 Dorsal venous arch

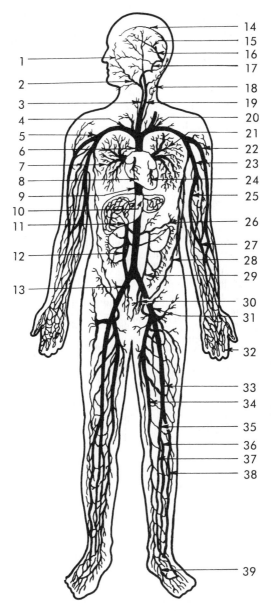

1
2
3
4
5
6
7
8
9
10
11
12
13

14
15
16
17
18
19
20
21
22
23
24
25
26
27
28
29
30
31
32
33
34
35
36
37
38

39

Figure 10-2 Principal veins of the body. (From Austrin MG, Austrin HR: *Learning medical terminology*, ed 9, St Louis, 1998, Mosby.)

CIRCULATION OF BLOOD THROUGH THE HEART

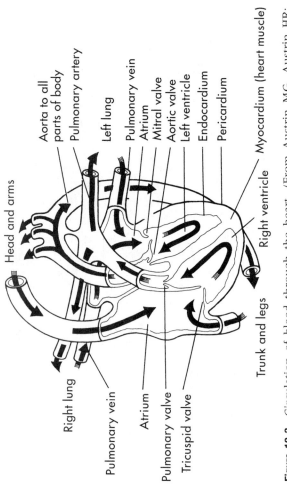

Figure 10-3 Circulation of blood through the heart. (From Austrin MG, Austrin HR: *Learning medical terminology*, ed 9, St Louis, 1998, Mosby.)

CORONARY ARTERIES
Right Coronary Artery
Right atrium and anterior right ventricle
Supplies blood to:
> Posterior septum (90%)
> Posterior papillary muscle
> Sinus and atrioventricular (AV) nodes (80%-90%)
> Inferior aspect of left ventricle

Left Coronary Artery
Left anterior descending (LAD)
Supplies blood to:
> Anterior left ventricular wall
> Anterior papillary muscle
> Left ventricular apex
> Anterior interventricular septum
>> Septal branches supply conduction system
>> System bundle of His and bundle branches

Circumflex
Supplies blood to:
> Left atrium
> Posterior surfaces of left ventricle
> Posterior aspect of the septum

BASIC CARDIAC ASSESSMENT

S_1

First heart sound—heard when the mitral and tricuspid valves close. After ventricles are filled with blood, a dull, low-pitched "lub" is heard. Systole begins when ventricles contract. Systole is shorter than diastole.

S_2

Second heart sound—heard when the aortic and pulmonic valves close. After blood goes to aorta and pulmonary artery, a high-pitched, snappy "dub" is heard.

CARDIAC HISTORY

Client History

Past heart attacks, rheumatic fever, fevers, hypertension, dizziness, syncope, diabetes, lung or endocrine diseases.

Health Habits

Smoking, alcohol, diet, exercise, stress.

Family History

Coronary disease, strokes, or obesity in parents or grandparents.

Signs and Symptoms

Chest pain, shortness of breath, orthopnea, syncope, hypertension, dyspnea, edema, cough, palpitations, wheezing, need for extra pillow to sleep, fatigue, weakness.

TOPOGRAPHIC AREAS FOR CARDIAC AUSCULTATION

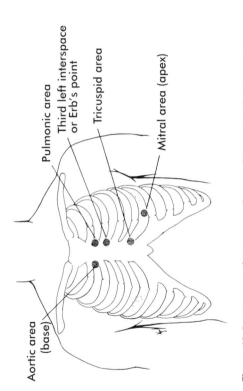

Figure 10-4   Topographic areas for cardiac auscultation. (From Phipps WJ, Long BC, Woods NF: *Medical-surgical nursing: concepts and clinical practice*, ed 6, St Louis, 1999, Mosby.)

Aortic area (base)

Pulmonic area

Third left interspace or Erb's point

Tricuspid area

Mitral area (apex)

ABNORMAL HEART SOUNDS

S_1 Varying intensity with different beats—indicates possible heart blockage

S_2 Increased intensity at aortic valve—indicates possible hypertension

S_3 Increased intensity at pulmonic valve—indicates possible hypertension

Systole Sharp sound—indicates possible deformity

Diastole Presence of S_3 in the elderly—indicates possible heart failure

S_1 S_2 S_3 "Ken tuck ky"

S_4 S_1 S_2 "Ten nes see"

PULSE GRADING SCALE

4-Point Scale	**3-Point Scale**
0 No pulse	0 Absent
1+ Weak, thready, fading, easily obliterated	1+ Weak, thready
2+ Difficult to palpate	2+ Normal
3+ Normal	3+ Full, bounding
4+ Bounding	

Cardiovascular Drugs		
Agent	Side Effects	Consideration
Digoxin (Lanoxin) (IV/PO)	Fatigue, headache, anoxia	Monitor rhythm and blood pressure during administration
Digitoxin (PO)	Arrhythmia, nausea, vomiting	Monitor heart rate and blood pressure
Nitroglycerin (IV/PO/buccal/ointment/ transdermal)	Headache, hypotension, nausea, vomiting, flushing, arrhythmia	Monitor for arrhythmia
Amrinone (IV)	Arrhythmia, hypotension, thrombocytopenia	Monitor rhythm, blood pressure, and heart rate
Milrinone (IV)	Arrhythmia, hypotension, thrombocytopenia	Monitor rhythm, blood pressure, and heart rate
Dobutamine (IV)	Tachycardia, angina, shortness of breath, headache, ventricular ectopy, nausea	Monitor output Monitor rhythm and blood pressure Check peripheral pulses

Continued

Cardiovascular Drugs—cont'd		
Agent	**Side Effects**	**Consideration**
Dopamine (IV)	Tachycardia, angina, shortness of breath, headache, ventricular ectopy, nausea	Monitor output Monitor rhythm and blood pressure
Epinephrine (IV)	Arrhythmia, hypertension, headache, hyperglycemia, nausea	Check peripheral pulses Monitor output Monitor rhythm and blood pressure Check peripheral pulses
Norepinephrine	Bradycardia, tachycardia, angina, headache, dizziness	Monitor rhythm and blood pressure Have atropine available Monitor fluid balance
Isoproterenol (IV)	Arrhythmia, hypertension, nausea, vomiting, flushing, headache	Monitor rhythm and blood pressure Monitor for arrhythmia Monitor fluid balance

ASSESSMENT OF PULSE SITES*

Temporal Found over the **temporal bone,** above and lateral to the eye; easily accessible, used often in children

Apical Best found between the **fourth and fifth intercostal space,** midclavicular line; used to auscultate heart sounds and before the administration of digoxin

Carotid Found on either side of the neck over the **carotid artery;** used to assess circulation during shock or cardiac arrest and when other peripheral pulses are poor

Brachial Found in the **antecubital area** of the arm; used to auscultate blood pressure and to assess circulation of the lower arm

Radial Found on the **thumb side of the forearm** at the wrist; used to assess circulation of the hand and peripheral circulation

Ulnar Found at the **wrist on the opposite side of the radius;** used to assess circulation of the hand and in Allen's assessment test

Femoral Found below the **inguinal ligament,** midway between the symphysis pubis and the anterosuperior iliac spine; used to assess circulation of the leg; can be used to assess circulation during shock or a cardiac arrest or when other peripheral pulses are poor

Popliteal Found **behind the knee;** used to assess lower leg circulation

Posterior tibial Found on the **inner side of each ankle;** used to assess foot circulation

Dorsalis pedis Found along the **top of the foot** between extension tendons of the great and first toes; used to assess the circulation of the foot

*See Figure 4-1, p. 95.

QUALITY AND PITCH OF MURMURS

Type	Quality	Pitch
Aortic and pulmonary stenosis	Harsh	Medium-high
Mitral and tricuspid regurgitation	Blowing	High
Ventricular septal defect	Usually harsh	High
Mitral stenosis	Rumbling	Low
Aortic regurgitation	Blowing	High

MURMUR GRADING SCALE

1 Difficult to hear
2 Faint but recognizable
3 Heard easily with stethoscope
4 Loud, often with a palpable thrill
5 Very loud; associated with a thrill
6 Stethoscope not needed to hear; can be heard with stethoscope 1 inch from chest

EDEMA GRADING SCALE

1+ Barely detectable
2+ Indentation of <5 mm
3+ Indentation of 5 to 10 mm
4+ Indentation of >10 mm

Tissue Perfusion		
Area	**Abnormality**	**Assessment**
Skin color	Cyanotic	Decreased venous return
	Pallor	Decreased arterial flow
	Dusky	Decreased arterial flow
Temperature	Cool	Decreased arterial flow
Fluid	Mild edema	Decreased arterial flow
	Great edema	Decreased venous return
Texture	Thin or thick	Decreased venous return and arterial flow
	Shiny	Decreased venous return and arterial flow
Nails	Cyanotic	Decreased arterial flow

Chapter 11

Respiratory System

For an in-depth study of the respiratory system,
consult the following publications:

Austrin MG, Austrin HR: *Learning medical terminology,* ed 9, St Louis, 1998,
     Mosby.
Guzzetta CE, Dossey BM: *Cardiovascular nursing: holistic practice,* St Louis,
     1992, Mosby.
Lewis SM, Collier IC, Heitkemper MM: *Medical-surgical nursing,* ed 5,
     St Louis, 2000, Mosby.
Patton KT, Thibodeau GA: *Handbook for anatomy and physiology,* St Louis,
     2000, Mosby.
Potter PA, Perry AG: *Fundamentals of nursing,* ed 5, St Louis, 2001, Mosby.

LOWER RESPIRATORY TRACT

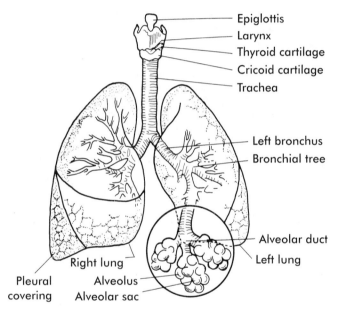

Figure 11-1   Lower respiratory tract. (From Austrin MG, Austrin HR: *Learning medical terminology,* ed 9, St Louis, 1998, Mosby.)

UPPER RESPIRATORY TRACT

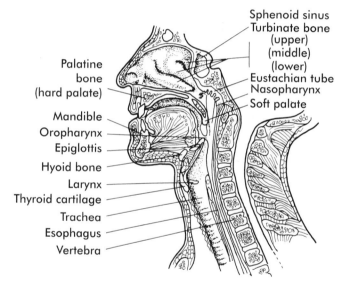

Figure 11-2   Upper respiratory tract. (From Austrin MG, Austrin HR: *Learning medical terminology*, ed 9, St Louis, 1998, Mosby.)

CHEST WALL LANDMARKS

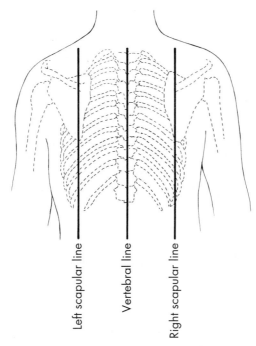

Figure 11-3 Chest wall landmarks. (From Potter PA, Perry AG: *Fundamentals of nursing,* ed 5, St Louis, 2001, Mosby.)

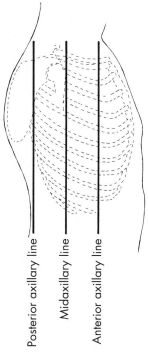

Figure 11-3, cont'd

Continued

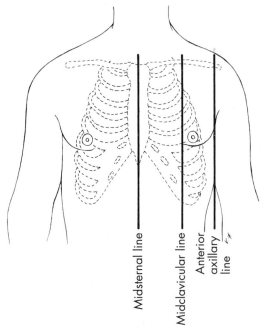

Figure 11-3, cont'd

NORMAL BREATH SOUNDS

Vesicular Soft, low-pitched sighing over bronchiole and alveoli bases on inspiration

Bronchial Moderate, high-pitched sound over trachea

Bronchovesicular Moderate sound over first and second intercostal spaces

Tracheal Loudest and highest pitched of normal breath sounds, harsh and tubular

SIGNS AND SYMPTOMS OF HYPERVENTILATION

Tachycardia, chest pain, shortness of breath

Dizziness, lightheadedness, disorientation

Paresthesia, numbness

Tinnitus, blurred vision, tetany

SIGNS AND SYMPTOMS OF HYPOVENTILATION

Dizziness, headache, lethargy

Disorientation, convulsions, coma

Decreased ability to follow instructions

Cardiac arrhythmias, electrolyte imbalance, cardiac arrest

SIGNS AND SYMPTOMS OF HYPOXIA

Restlessness, anxiety, disorientation

Decreased concentration, fatigue

Decreased consciousness, dizziness

Behavioral changes, pallor

Increased pulse and blood pressure

Cardiac arrhythmias, cyanosis, clubbing, dyspnea

Common Abnormalities of the Lung

Type	Characteristics	Assess for
Apnea	Periods of not breathing	Sleep problem, impending death
Bradypnea	<10 breaths per minute	Drug overdose, alcohol overdose
Dyspnea	Difficulty breathing	Low hemoglobin, acidosis
Stridor	High-pitched sounds	Obstruction
Tachypnea	>20 breaths per minute	Anxiety, fever
Hyperpnea	Increased rate and depth	Pain, reaction to altitude
Hyperventilation	Increased rate and depth	Acidosis
Cheyne-Stokes breathing	Alternating periods of hyperpnea and apnea	Impending death
Kussmaul respirations	Extreme rate and depth	Diabetic ketoacidosis, renal failure
Asymmetric	Lungs do not expand equally	Fractured ribs, missing lung, pneumothorax

ABNORMAL AND ADVENTITIOUS SOUNDS

Crackles/rales Fine, cracklelike sounds, usually on inspiration

Alveolar High pitched

Bronchial Low pitched

Rhonchi Coarse, harsh, over fluid (usually on expiration)

Wheezes Squeaky, musical on inspiration or expiration

Friction rub Grating sound of pleurae rubbing together, generally on the anterior side

COMMON LUNG DISORDERS
Asthma
Signs and Symptoms. Dyspnea, cough, tachypnea.
Listen for. Decreased sounds with wheezes.

Atelectasis
Signs and Symptoms. Tachypnea, cyanosis, use of accessory muscles.
Listen for. Decreased sound with crackles.

Bronchitis
Signs and Symptoms. Cough with sputum, sore throat and fever, prolonged expiration.
Listen for. Prolonged expiration, wheezes, crackles.

Emphysema
Signs and Symptoms. Dyspnea, cough with sputum.
Listen for. Wheezes, rhonchi.

Neoplasm
Signs and Symptoms. Cough with sputum, possible chest pain.
Listen for. Decreased sounds.

Pleural Effusion
Signs and Symptoms. Pain, dyspnea, pallor, fever, cough.
Listen for. Decreased sounds, friction rub.

Pneumonia
Signs and Symptoms. Chills, productive cough, rapid swallow rate.
Listen for. Fine crackles or friction rub.

Pneumothorax
Signs and Symptoms. Pain, dyspnea, cyanosis, tachypnea.
Listen for. Decreased sound on affected side.

Pulmonary Edema
Signs and Symptoms. Tachypnea, cough, cyanosis, orthopnea, use of accessory muscles.
Listen for. Rales, rhonchi, wheezes.

Positions for Postural Drainage

Lung Segment	Position of Client
Adult	
Bilateral	High Fowler's

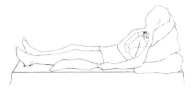

Apical segments Right upper lobe— anterior segment	Supine with head elevated

Left upper lobe— anterior segment	Supine with head elevated

Modified from Potter PA, Perry AG: *Fundamentals of nursing,* ed 5, St Louis, 2001, Mosby.

Positions for Postural Drainage—cont'd

Lung Segment	**Position of Client**
Right upper lobe— posterior segment	Side lying with right side of chest elevated on pillows

Left upper lobe— posterior segment	Side lying with left side of chest elevated on pillows

Right middle lobe— anterior segment	Three-fourths supine position with dependent lung in Trendelenburg position

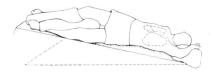

Continued

Positions for Postural Drainage—cont'd

Lung Segment	Position of Client
Right middle lobe— posterior segment	Prone with thorax and abdomen elevated

| Both lower lobes— anterior segments | Supine in Trendelenburg position |

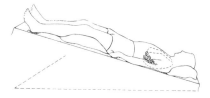

| Left lower lobe— lateral segment | Right side lying in Trendelenburg position |

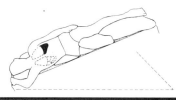

Modified from Potter PA, Perry AG: *Fundamentals of nursing,* ed 5, St Louis, 2001, Mosby.

Positions for Postural Drainage—cont'd

Lung Segment	Position of Client
Right lower lobe—lateral segment	Left side lying in Trendelenburg position

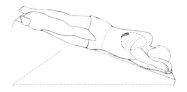

Right lower lobe—posterior segment	Prone with right side of chest elevated in Trendelenburg position

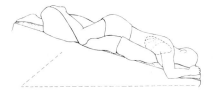

Both lower lobes—posterior segment	Prone in Trendelenburg position

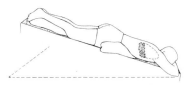

Continued

Positions for Postural Drainage—cont'd

Lung Segment	Position of Client

Child

Bilateral—apical segments

Sitting on nurse's lap, leaning slightly forward flexed over pillow

Bilateral—middle anterior segments

Sitting on nurse's lap, leaning against nurse

Bilateral lobes— anterior segments

Lying supine on nurse's lap, back supported with pillow

Modified from Potter PA, Perry AG: *Fundamentals of nursing,* ed 5, St Louis, 2001, Mosby.

OXYGEN THERAPY*
Cannula
1 liter = 24% oxygen
2 liters = 28% oxygen
3 liters = 32% oxygen
4 liters = 36% oxygen
5 liters = 40% oxygen
6 liters = 44% oxygen

If client requires more oxygen than 6 liters, a mask may be needed. Humidification may be added for comfort.

Simple Mask
5-6 liters = 40% oxygen
7-8 liters = 50% oxygen
 10 liters = 60% oxygen

Should not be run below 5 liters per minute.

Partial Rebreathing Mask
6-10 liters = up to 80% oxygen

Level of oxygen will depend on client's overall respiratory and health status. *Should not be run below 5 liters per minute. Reservoir bag should never be fully collapsed.*

Nonbreathing Mask
Will deliver 80% to 100% oxygen. *Should not be run below 5 liters per minute. Reservoir bag should never be fully collapsed.*

*Oxygen is a drug, and therefore a physician's order is required for use.

Pulmonary Functions

Name	Description	Average	Considerations
Tidal volume (VT)	Amount of air inhaled or exhaled	5-10 ml/kg	Decreased in older adults and clients with restrictive lung disease
Residual volume (RV)	Amount of air left in lung after deep exhalation	1200 ml	Increased in clients with chronic obstructive pulmonary disease
Functional residual capacity (FRC)	Air left in lung after normal exhalation	2400 ml	Increased in clients with obstructive lung diseases
Vital capacity (VC)	Amount of air exhaled after maximal inhalation	4800 ml	Decreased with pulmonary edema and atelectasis
Total lung capacity (TLC)	Total air in lungs after maximal inhalation	6000 ml	Decreased with restrictive disease Increased with obstructive disease

Chapter 12

Endocrine System

For an in-depth study of the endocrine system,
consult the following publications:

AJN/Mosby: *Nursing boards review for the NCLEX-RN examination,* ed 10,
St Louis, 1996, Mosby.

Lewis SM, Collier IC, Heitkemper MM: *Medical-surgical nursing,* ed 5,
St Louis, 2000, Mosby.

Phipps WJ, Sands JK, Marek JF: *Medical-surgical nursing: concepts and
clinical practice,* ed 6, St Louis, 1999, Mosby.

Potter PA, Perry AG: *Fundamentals of nursing,* ed 5, St Louis, 2001, Mosby.

ENDOCRINE GLANDS AND ASSOCIATED STRUCTURES

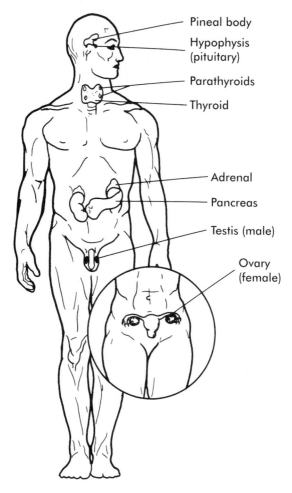

Figure 12-1 Endocrine glands. (From Austrin MG, Austrin HR: *Learning medical terminology,* ed 9, St Louis, 1998, Mosby.)

DIABETES

Type 1 (IDDM) **Insulin Dependent**	Type 2 (NIDDM) **Non-Insulin Dependent**
Clinical Information	
10% to 15% of diabetic cases	85% to 90% of diabetic cases
Abrupt onset	Gradual onset
Autoimmune islet-cell destruction	Insulin resistance or deficiency
Generally begins before age 40 years but can occur at any age	Generally begins after age 40 years but can occur earlier
Clinical Manifestations	
Weight loss, increased hunger	Fatigue, drowsiness, increased hunger
Excessive thirst, increased urinary frequency	Blurred vision, increased thirst, urinary frequency
Possible ketoacidosis	No ketoacidosis
Prone to ketosis	No ketosis
No endogenous insulin	Has endogenous insulin
Diet very important	Diet very important
Insulin mandatory	Insulin needed in 25% of cases
Oral hypoglycemic not used	Oral hypoglycemic used in 40% of cases

BLOOD GLUCOSE REACTIONS

Insulin Reaction	**Diabetic Ketoacidosis**
Hypoglycemia	**Hyperglycemia**
(Glucose Level	**(Glucose Level**
<60 mg/dl)	**>250 mg/dl)**

Causes	*Causes*
Too much insulin	Too little insulin
Skipped or delayed meals	Overeating
Too much exercise	Emotional stress, illness, infection, surgery, heart attack, stroke, pregnancy

Clinical Manifestations

Early Symptoms	*Early Symptoms*
Sweatiness, shakiness, weakness	Excessive thirst
Headache, dizziness	Frequent urination
Hunger	Fatigue, weakness

Late Symptoms	*Late Symptoms*
Numbness of lips/tongue	Abdominal pain, nausea, vomiting
Difficulty concentrating	General aches, loss of appetite
Mood change/irritability	Flushed, dry skin
Vision changes, pallor	Fruity breath, drowsiness

If Not Treated	*If Not Treated*
Seizures, coma	Labored breathing, coma

TREATMENT FOR BLOOD GLUCOSE REACTIONS

Insulin Reaction
Hypoglycemia
(Glucose Level
<60 mg/dl)

One of the Following:
10 to 15 g glucose or
  2 glucose tablets
5 pieces of candy or
  4 oz juice
1 mg IM glucagon
Repeat any *one* of the
  above in 15 minutes
  if needed
Document reaction
Inform physician

Diabetic Ketoacidosis
Hyperglycemia
(Glucose Level
>250 mg/dl)

Complete the Following:
Alert physician
Monitor blood sugar
Test urine for ketones
Provide IV hydration
  per physician's orders
Provide potassium
  replacements
Give insulin per physician's
  order
Document actions

RECOMMENDATIONS FOR MIXING INSULINS

When mixing short- and long-acting insulins in the same syringe, first draw up the short-acting insulin (regular insulin, which is clear) and then the long-acting insulin (which is cloudy).

- Clients whose blood sugar levels are well controlled on a mixed-insulin dose should maintain their individual routine.
- Insulin should not mixed with other medications.
- Insulin should not be diluted unless approved by the prescribing physician.
- Rapid-acting insulins that are mixed with NPH or Ultralente insulins should be injected 15 minutes before a meal to promote consistent absorption of insulin.
- Short-acting and Lente insulins should not be mixed unless the client's blood sugar level is currently under control with this mixture.

Modified from American Diabetes Association: Clinical practice recommendations for insulin administration, *Diabetes Care* 20(suppl 1):46s, 1997.

REACTION PREVENTION TIPS

Insulin Reaction	**Diabetic Ketoacidosis**
Eat meals at same time each day	Follow prescribed eating schedule

If meals are delayed:
  For 1 hour: Drink 4 oz fruit juice
  For more than 2 hours: Eat 4 oz protein
	Know factors that can raise blood sugar
	Avoid stress and overwork

Take correct insulin as scheduled	Take correct insulin as scheduled
Wear diabetic identification	Wear diabetic identification

Check blood sugar as needed	On sick days:
	  Do not stop insulin
	  Check urine for ketones every 12 hours
	  Monitor blood glucose every 2 to 4 hours
	  Maintain good fluid intake
	  Alert physician if glucose is >240 mg/dl

Carry quick-acting sugar at all times	

General Client and Family Information

With an increase in activity, never omit insulin.

Before vacations, call physician to see whether insulin dose needs adjusting.

Know insulin peaks and how body reacts to insulin highs and lows.

Inform family and friends of possible reactions and how to treat them.

Hypoglycemic Agents*		
Types	Peak (hr)	Duration (hr)
Oral agents		
Chlorpropamide (Diabinese)	1	24-60
Tolbutamide (Orinase)	5-8	6-12
Tolazamide (Tolinase)	4-6	12-24
Glipizide (Glucotrol)	1-3	10-24
Glyburide (DiaBeta, Micronase, Glynase Prestab)	2-8	24
Acarbose (Precose)	1	14-24
Acetohexamide (Dymelor)	1.3-8	12-24
Glimepiride (Amaryl)	2-3	24
Metformin hydrochloride (Glucophage)	1-3	9-17
Miglitol (Glyset)	2-3	24
Nateglinide (Starlix)	0-1	2-3
Repaglinide (Prandin)	60-90 min	<4

Insulin
Rapid acting (onset 1 hr)

Regular	2-4	4-12
Insulin zinc (Semilente)	5-10	12-16
Regular human (Humulin-R, Novolin-R)	1-3	3-5

Intermediate acting (onset 2-4 hr)

Globin zinc (Iletin)	6-10	18-24
Isophane suspension (NPH)	4-12	18-24
Insulin zinc suspension (Iletin Lente)	7-15	18-24
NPH human isophane (Humulin-N, Novolin-N)	8-12	26-30

Long acting (onset 4-6 hr)

Protamine zinc (PZ)	14-24	24-36
Insulin zinc extended (Ultralente)	10-30	>36
Insulin glargine (Lantus)	n/a	24

Data from *Drug facts & comparisons*, St. Louis, 2002, Facts & Comparisons; *Physicians' desk reference*, ed 54, Montvale, NJ, 2000, Medical Economics.
*New oral agents are being developed constantly. This is a partial listing.

ADRENAL GLANDS

Cushing's Syndrome Hyperfunction	Addison's Disease Hypofunction
Clinical Manifestations	
Excessive cortisol production	Inadequate cortisol production
Increased ACTH from pituitary	Insufficient ACTH from pituitary
Increased protein catabolism	Flaccid muscles/paralysis
Muscle wasting and fragile skin	Muscle weakness and anorexia
Osteoporosis and compression fractures	Nausea/vomiting and diarrhea
Bruises easily/poor healing	Abdominal pain
Obesity/moon face/ buffalo hump	Weight loss
Hyperglycemia and worsening of diabetes	Frequent hypoglycemia
Decreased immunity	Decreased cardiac output
Sodium and water retention	Hyponatremia and hypo-osmolality
Edema/hypertension	Hypotension and arrhythmias
Hypokalemia/ hypochloremia	Hyperkalemia
Renal calculi hypercalcemia	Hypercalcemia
Irritability	Lethargy
Anxiety	Depression

PITUITARY GLAND*

Hyperpituitarism

Clinical Information. This disorder is generally caused by tumors, which lead to an increase in hormone levels. The most common hormones involved are the following:

GH Growth hormone, which causes gigantism

ACTH Adrenocorticotropic hormone (corticotropin), which causes Cushing's disease

TSH Thyroid-stimulating hormone, which causes hyperthyroidism

LH Luteinizing hormone

FSH Follicle-stimulating hormone

Hypopituitarism

Clinical Information. This disorder is usually caused by tumors, necrosis, or glandular dysfunction, leading to a decrease in hormone levels. The most common problems associated with hypopituitarism are:

Dwarfism Caused by a decreased growth hormone

Hypophysectomy The removal or destruction of pituitary gland

Postpartum necrosis Caused by hypotension after delivery

Functional disorders Caused by starvation or anemia

*Specific problems, signs, and symptoms will depend on the hormone involved.

THYROID GLAND

Hyperthyroidism	**Hypothyroidism**
Clinical Manifestations	
Increased body metabolism	Decreased body metabolism
Nervousness/restlessness	Lethargy and headaches
Short attention span	Memory deficit
Tachycardia (>100 beats/min; bounding heart sounds)	Bradycardia (<60 beats/min; weak heart sounds)
Increased blood pressure	Decreased blood pressure
Reduced vital capacity	Lowered respiratory rate
Skin warm, moist, and smooth	Skin cool, dry, and rough
Hair fine, nails soft	Hair coarse, nails brittle
Weakness and fatigue	Weakness and fatigue
Demineralization of bones	Stiff joints
Hypercalcemia	Mild proteinuria
Brisk reflexes	Decreased reflexes
Increased appetite/weight loss	Decreased appetite/weight gain
Muscle wasting	Muscular stiffness
Diabetes worsens	Diabetic clients need less insulin
Increased stools	Constipation
Increased libido	Decreased libido
Decreased fertility	Decreased fertility
Higher body temperature	Lower body temperature

Chapter 13

 Digestive System

For in-depth study of the digestive system,
consult the following publications:

AJN/Mosby: *Nursing boards review for the NCLEX-RN examination,* ed 10,
     St Louis, 1996, Mosby.
Lewis SM, Collier IC, Heitkemper MM: *Medical-surgical nursing,* ed 5,
     St Louis, 2000, Mosby.
Phipps WJ, Sands JK, Marek JF: *Medical-surgical nursing: concepts and
     clinical practice,* ed 6, St Louis, 1999, Mosby.
Potter PA, Perry AG: *Fundamentals of nursing,* ed 5, St Louis, 2001, Mosby.
Williams SR: *Basic nutrition and diet therapy,* ed 11, St Louis, 2000, Mosby.

DIGESTIVE SYSTEM AND ASSOCIATED STRUCTURES

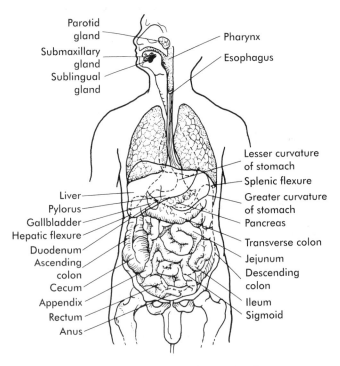

Figure 13-1 Digestive system and associated structures. (From Austrin MG, Austrin HR: *Learning medical terminology*, ed 9, St Louis, 1998, Mosby.)

Types of Diets

Type	Description	Client Complaint
Regular	Has all essentials, no restrictions	No special diet needed
Clear liquid	Broth, tea, clear soda, strained juices, gelatin	Recovery from surgery or very ill
Full liquid	Clear liquids plus milk products, eggs	Transition from clear to regular diet
Soft	Soft consistency and mild spice	Difficulty swallowing
Mechanical soft	Regular diet but chopped or ground	Difficulty chewing
Bland	No spicy food	Ulcers or colitis
Low residue	No bulky food, apples, or nuts	Rectal disease
High calorie	High protein, vitamin, and fat	Malnourished
Low calorie	Decreased fat, no whole milk, cream, eggs, complex carbohydrates	Obese

Continued

	Types of Diets—cont'd	
Type	Description	Client Complaint
Diabetic	Balance of protein, carbohydrates, fat	Insulin-food imbalance
High protein	Meat, fish, milk, cheese, poultry, eggs	Tissue repair, underweight
Low fat	Little butter, cream, whole milk, or eggs	Gallbladder, liver, or heart disease
Low cholesterol	Little meat or cheese	Need to decrease fat intake
Low sodium	No salt added during cooking	Heart or renal disease
Salt free	No salt	Heart or renal disease
Tube feeding	Formulas or liquid food	Oral surgery, oral or esophageal cancers, inability to eat or swallow

Types of Nutrients		
Type	**Function**	**Food Sources**
Carbohydrate	Energy, body temperature	*Simple:* sugars, fruits, nuts *Complex:* grains, potatoes, milk
Protein	Tissue growth, tissue repair	Meat, fish, eggs, milk, poultry, beans, peas, nuts
Fat	Energy and repair, carries vitamins A and D	Animal fat, meat, nuts, milk, fish, poultry
Water	Carries nutrients, regulates body processes, lubricates joints	Liquids, most fruits and vegetables

Minerals		
Type	Function	Food Sources
Calcium	Renews bones and teeth, regulates heart and nerves	Milk, green vegetables, cheese, salmon, legumes
Phosphorus	Renews bones and teeth, maintains nerve function	Cheese, oats, meat, milk, fish, poultry, nuts
Iron	Renews hemoglobin	Meat, eggs, liver, flour, yellow or green vegetables
Iodine	Regulates thyroid	Table salt, seafood
Magnesium	Component of enzymes	Grains, green vegetables
Sodium	Maintains water balance, nerve function	Salt, cured meats
Potassium	Maintains nerve function	Meat, milk, vegetables
Chloride	Formation of gastric juices	Salt
Zinc	Component of enzymes	Meat, seafood

	Vitamins	
Type	**Function**	**Food Sources**
A (retinol)	Helps eyes, skin, hair; fights infection	Yellow fruits and vegetables, liver, kidneys, fish
B_1 (thiamine)	Maintains nerves, aids carbohydrate function	Bread, cereal, beans, peas, pork, liver, eggs, milk
B_2 (riboflavin)	Maintains skin, mouth, nerve functions	Milk, cheese, eggs, cereal, dark green vegetables
B_3 (niacin)	Oxidation of proteins and carbohydrates	Meat, fish, poultry, eggs, nuts, bread, cereal
B_{12}	Aids muscles, nerves, heart, metabolism	Organ meats, milk
C (ascorbic acid)	Maintains integrity of cells, repairs tissue	Citrus fruits, tomatoes, green vegetables, potatoes
D	Enables body to use calcium and phosphorus	Milk, margarine, fish, liver, eggs
E	Antioxidant	Peanuts, vegetable oils
K	Aids in blood clotting	Green leafy vegetables

CALORIC INCREASE NEEDED FOR SELECT INJURY FACTORS

Injury	% Caloric Increase
Minor surgery	10
Mild infection	20
Moderate infection	40
Severe infection	60
Congestive heart failure	30
Cancer therapy	30
Pulmonary disease	30
Wound healing	20-60
Long bone fracture	30-50

Modified from Kobriger Presents. www.kobriger.com

TWO TYPES OF MALNUTRITION

Marasmus
Caused by decreased caloric intake
- Takes months to years to develop
- Individuals appear thin, malnourished
- Weight loss present
- Serum albumin and transferrin levels normal
- Mortality rate low, unless from underlying disease

Kwashiorkor
Caused by decreased protein intake or stress
- Can be due to trauma or infection
- Takes only weeks to develop
- Individuals appear normal, well nourished
- Weight loss may be minimal or masked by edema
- Serum albumin and transferrin levels decreased
- Mortality rate high due to decreased wound healing
- High risk of infection

Modified from Kobriger Presents. www.kobriger.com

COMPARING PEPTIC ULCERS

Gastric Ulcers	Duodenal Ulcers
Located in the antum of stomach	Located in the first 1 to 2 cm of the duodenum
Generally occurs in people aged 45 to 70 years	Generally occurs in people aged 40 to 60 years
Most common ulcer in people >65 years old	Most common ulcer in people <65 years old
More common in women	More common in men
Higher mortality rate than duodenal ulcers	Lower mortality rate than gastric ulcers
Less common than duodenal ulcers	Four times more prevalent than gastric ulcers
Risk factors are stress, drugs, alcohol, smoking, and gastritis	Risk factors are chronic obstructive pulmonary disease, alcohol, cirrhosis, pancreatitis, smoking, renal failure, stress
Pain occurs 1 to 2 hours after eating	Pain occurs after eating and at night
Pain felt high in epigastrium	Pain in midepigastric area
Pain may be described as heartburn	Pain is described in the back
Pain relieved by food or liquids	Pain relieved by milk or antacids
May cause weight loss	May cause weight gain
High recurrence rate	Recurs seasonally (spring/fall)
Risk of malignancy	Rarely malignant
High risk of hemorrhage	High risk of perforation

ALTERED BOWEL ELIMINATION PATTERNS

Constipation

Presence of large quantity of dry, hard feces that is difficult to expel; frequency of bowel movements is not a factor.

Causes. Reabsorption of too much water in the lower bowel as a result of medications such as narcotics, ignoring the urge to defecate, immobility, chronic laxative abuse, low fluid intake, low fiber intake, aging, postoperative conditions, or pregnancy.

Remedies. Increase fluids, fiber cereals, fruits and vegetables, and exercise and avoid cheese.

Impaction

Hard, dry stool embedded in rectal folds; may have liquid stool passing around impaction.

Causes. Poor bowel habits, immobility, inadequate food or fluids, or barium in rectum.

Remedies. Digitally remove impaction, increase fluids and fiber, increase exercise, and institute bowel program.

Diarrhea

Expulsion of fecal matter that contains too much water.

Causes. Infection, anxiety, stress, medications, too many laxatives at one time, or food or drug allergies or reactions.

Remedies. Add bulk or fiber to diet, maintain fluids and electrolytes, eat smaller amounts of food at one time, add cheese or bananas to diet, and rest after eating.

Incontinence

Inability to hold feces in rectum because of impairment of sphincter control.

Causes. Surgery, cancer, radiation treatment of rectum, paralysis, or aging.

Remedies. Bowel training, regular meal times, regular elimination patterns.

Abdominal Distention

Tympanites, or enlargement of the abdomen with gas or air as a result of excessive swallowing of air, eating gas-producing foods, or an inability to expel gas.

Causes. Constipation, fecal impaction, or postoperative conditions.

Remedies. Rectal tube can be used to expel air; increase ambulation, and change position in bed.

Obstruction

Occurs when the lumen of the bowel narrows or closes completely.

Causes. External compression can be caused by tumor; internal narrowing can be caused by impacted feces.

Remedies. Remove impaction or tumor.

Ileus (Paralytic Ileus)

Occurs when the bowel has decreased motility.

Causes. Surgery, long-term narcotic use, or complete obstruction.

Remedies. Medical intervention for physical obstructions. Specific action will depend on the cause of the ileus.

Fecal Characteristics

Characteristic	Normal	Abnormal	Assess for
Color	Brown	Clay/white	Bile obstruction
		Black/tarry	Upper GI bleeding, iron
		Red	Lower GI bleeding, beets
		Pale	Malabsorption of fat
		Green	Infection
Consistency	Moist	Hard	Constipation, dehydration
	Formed	Loose	Diet, diarrhea, medications
		Watery	Infection
		Liquid	Impaction
Odor	Aromatic	Pungent	Infection, blood
Frequency	1-2 times per day	5 times per day	Infection, diet
	Once every 3 days	Once every 6 days	Constipation, activity, medications
Shape	Cylindric	Narrow, "ribbon-like"	Obstruction

FOODS AND THEIR EFFECT ON FECAL OUTPUT

To thicken stool, a person should eat:
Bananas, rice, bread, potatoes
Creamy peanut butter, applesauce
Cheese, yogurt, pasta, pretzels
Tapioca, marshmallows

To loosen stool, a person should eat:
Chocolate, raw fruits and vegetables
Spiced foods, greasy or fried foods
Prunes, grapes, leafy green vegetables

To decrease gas, a person should avoid:
Beans, beer, sodas
Cucumbers, cabbage, onions, spinach
Brussels sprouts, broccoli, cauliflower
Most dairy products, corn, radishes

TYPES OF CATHARTICS

Bulk-forming Increases fluids and bulk in the intestines, which stimulates peristalsis. An increase in fluid is needed.
Example: Metamucil

Emollient Softens and delays drying of stool.
Example: Liquid petrolatum

Irritant Stimulates peristalsis by irritating bowel mucosa and decreasing water absorption.
Example: Castor oil

Moistening (stool softeners) Increase water in the bowel.
Example: Colace

Saline When salt is in the bowel, the water will remain in the bowel as well. (Avoid use in clients with impaired renal function.)
Example: Milk of magnesia (MOM), Epsom salts

Suppository Stimulates bowel and softens stool.

ANTIDIARRHEAL MEDICATIONS

Absorbent Absorbs gas
Astringent Shrinks inflamed tissues
Demulcent Coats and protects bowel

TYPES OF ENEMAS

Carminative Used to expel flatus.

Cleansing Stimulates peristalsis; irritates bowel by distention. (Use 1 liter of fluid; have client hold it as long as possible.)

Colonic irrigation Used to expel flatus.

Hypertonic Phosphates irritate bowel and draw fluid into bowel through osmosis (90 to 120 ml—hold 10 to 15 minutes).

Hypotonic Tap water (1 liter—hold 15 minutes). Avoid with cardiac clients.

Medicated Contains a therapeutic agent (e.g., Kayexalate to treat high potassium levels).

Retention Oil given to soften stool (hold for 1 hour).

Saline Draws fluid into the bowel (9 ml of sodium to 1 liter of water—hold 15 minutes).

Soapsuds Irritates and distends bowel (5 ml of soap to 1 liter of water—hold 15 minutes). Use only castile soaps.

COMMON TYPES OF OSTOMIES*
Ileostomy
Effluent. A continuous discharge that is soft and wet. The output is somewhat odorous and contains intestinal enzymes that are irritating to peristomal skin.

Skin Barrier Option. Highly desirable for peristomal skin protection.

Pouch Option. Pouch necessary at all times.

Type of Pouch. Drainable or closed-end for specific needs.

Need for Irrigation. None.

*Illustrations on pp. 267-272 are from *The professional's guide to ostomy patients.* Used with permission of Convatec, a Bristol-Myers Squibb Co. Text discussion of common types of ostomies is also based on the preceding source.

Transverse Colostomy

Effluent. Usually semiliquid or very soft. Occasionally, transverse colostomy discharge is firm. Output is usually malodorous and can irritate peristomal skin. Double-barreled colostomies have two openings. Loop colostomies have one opening, but two tracks—the active (proximal), which discharges fecal matter, and the inactive (distal), with a mucus discharge.

Skin Barrier Option. Highly desirable for peristomal skin protection.

Pouch Option. Pouch necessary at all times.

Type of Pouch. Drainable or closed-end for specific needs.

Need for Irrigation. None.

Double-barreled colostomy   Loop colostomy

Descending Colostomy/Sigmoid Colostomy

Effluent. Semisolid from descending colostomy. Firm from sigmoid colostomy. On discharge, there is an odor. Discharge is irritating if left in contact with skin around stoma. Frequency of output is unpredictable and varies with each person.

Skin Barrier Option. May be used for peristomal skin protection if pouch is worn.

Pouch Option. Pouch should be worn if person does not irrigate.

Type of Pouch. Dramable, closed-end, or stoma cap.

Need for Irrigation. Yes, as instructed by enterostomal (ET) nurse or physician.

Descending colostomy Sigmoid colostomy

Urinary Diversion (Ileal Loop, Ileal, or Colonic Conduit)

Effluent. Urine only. Output is constant. Mucus is expelled with urine. Mild odor unless there is a urinary tract infection. Urine is irritating when in contact with skin. Segment of ileum or colon is used to construct stoma.

Skin Barrier Option. Highly desirable for peristomal skin protection.

Pouch Option. Pouch necessary at all times.

Type of Pouch. Drainable pouch with spout.

Need for Irrigation. None.

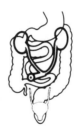

Continent Ileostomy

Effluent. Fluid bowel secretions are collected in a reservoir surgically constructed out of the lower part of the small intestine. Gas and feces are emptied via a surgically created leak-free nipple valve through which a catheter is inserted into the reservoir. For maximum efficiency and comfort, reservoir is usually emptied four or five times daily. Daily schedule for catheterization should be recommended by enterostomal (ET) nurse or physician.

Skin Barrier Option. None. An absorbent pad will provide peristomal skin protection.

Pouch Option. None—but catheter should be available at all times.

Type of Pouch. None. A drainable pouch can be applied if there is leakage of stool between intubations.

Need for Irrigation. Occasionally to liquify thick fecal matter, the pouch can be irrigated with 1 to 1½ oz of saline or water. Specific care should be clarified by enterostomal (ET) nurse or physician.

Continent Urostomy

Effluent. Urine is maintained in a surgically constructed ileal pouch until emptied by means of a catheter inserted into the stoma. Uses two nipple valves—one to prevent the reflux of urine from backing up into the kidneys, the other to keep urine in the pouch until eliminated. Pouch is drained approximately four times daily. Daily schedule for pouch catheterization should be recommended by ET nurse or physician.

Skin Barrier Option. None. An absorbent pad will provide peristomal skin protection.

Pouch Option. None—but a catheter should be available at all times.

Type of Pouch. None. A urostomy pouch can be applied if there is leakage of urine between intubations.

Need for Irrigation. Irrigate daily with 1 to 1½ oz of saline solution and repeat several times as needed until the returns are clear. Specific care should be clarified by enterostomal (ET) nurse or physician.

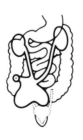

Chapter 14

 # Urinary System

For an in-depth study of the urinary system,
consult the following publications:

AJN/Mosby: *Nursing boards review for the NCLEX-RN examination,* ed 10,
    St Louis, 1996, Mosby.
Austrin MG, Austrin HR: *Learning medical terminology,* ed 9, St Louis, 1998.
Patton KT, Thibodeau GA: *Handbook for anatomy and physiology,* St Louis,
    2000, Mosby.
Phipps, WJ, Sands JK, Marek JF: *Medical-surgical nursing: concepts and
    clinical practice,* ed 6, St Louis, 1999, Mosby.
Potter PA, Perry AG: *Fundamentals of nursing,* ed 5, St Louis, 2001, Mosby.

ORGANS OF THE URINARY SYSTEM

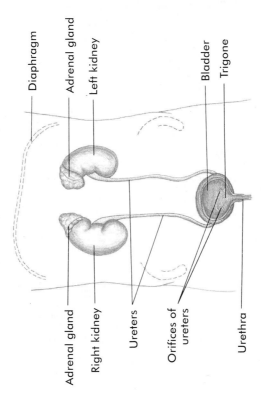

Figure 14-1 Organs of the urinary system. (From Potter PA, Perry AG: *Fundamentals of nursing*, ed 5, St Louis, 2001, Mosby.)

Altered Urinary Patterns

Pattern	Description	Assess for
Anuria	No urination	Renal failure, dehydration, obstruction
Dysuria	Painful urination	Infection, injury, frequency, blood
Frequency	Voiding small amounts	Infection, injury, pregnancy, stress, intake
Incontinence	Difficulty with control	Infection, injury, distended bladder
Nocturia	Urinating at night	Infection, injury, pregnancy, stress, intake
Oliguria	Little urination	Infection, injury, BUN, dehydration, kidney, disease
Polyuria	Increased urination	Infection, injury, alcohol, diabetes, caffeine, diuretics, increased thirst, dehydration
Retention	Holding on to urine	Infection, injury, pain, distended bladder, medications, restlessness, surgical complications
	No urination	
Residual	Urine remaining in bladder after voiding	Infection, distention, pain, injury
Urgency	Urgent and immediate need to void	Infection

Urinary Incontinence			
Type	Description	Causes	Symptoms
Function	Involuntary and unpredictable with intact urinary and nervous systems	Changes in environment or cognitive deficits	Urge to void that causes loss of urine
Reflex	Involuntary and occurring at predictable intervals	Anesthesia, medications, spinal cord dysfunction	Lack of urge to void
Stress	Intraabdominal pressure causes leakage	Coughing, laughing, obesity, pregnancy, weak muscles	Urgency and frequency
Urge	Involuntary passage of urine with strong urgency	Small bladder capacity, bladder irritation, alcohol, caffeine	Bladder spasms, urgency and frequency
Total	Uncontrolled and continuous loss of urine	Neuropathy, trauma, fistula between bladder and vagina	Constant flow, nocturia Unaware of incontinence

Urine Characteristics

Characteristics	Normal	Abnormal	Assess for
Amount in 24 hr	1200 ml	<1200 ml	Renal failure
	1500 ml	>1500 ml	Fluid intake
Color	Straw	Amber	Dehydration, fluid intake
		Light straw	Overhydration
		Orange	Medications
		Red	Blood, injury, medications
Consistency	Clear	Cloudy, thick	Infection
Odor	Faint	Offensive	Infection, medications
Sterile	Yes	Organisms	Infection, poor hygiene
pH	4.5	<4.5	Infection
	8.0	>8.0	Diabetes, starvation, dehydration
Specific gravity	1.010	<1.010	Diabetes insipidus, kidney failure
	1.025	>1.025	Diabetes, underhydration
Glucose	None	Present	Diabetes
Ketones	None	Present	Diabetes, starvation, vomiting
Blood	None	Present	Tumors, injury, kidney disease

MEDICATIONS THAT MAY DISCOLOR URINE
Dark Yellow
- Vitamin B$_2$

Orange
- Sulfonamide
- Phenazopyridine HCl (Pyridium)
- Warfarin (Coumadin)

Pink or Red
- Thorazine
- Ex-Lax
- Phenytoin (Dilantin)

Green or Blue
- Amitriptyline
- Methylene blue
- Triamterene (Dyrenium)

Brown or Black
- Iron
- Levodopa
- Nitrofurantoin
- Metronidazole (Flagyl)

REASONS FOR URINARY CATHETERS
Intermittent
- Relieve bladder distention
- Obtain a sterile specimen
- Assessment of residual urine
- Long-term management of spinal cord clients

Short-Term Indwelling
- After surgery
- Prevention of urethral obstruction
- Measurement of output in bedridden clients
- Bladder irrigation

Long-Term Indwelling
- Severe urinary retention
- Avoidance of skin rashes or infections

TYPES AND SIZES OF URINARY CATHETERS

Type	Size
Single lumen	8F to 18F (French*)
Double lumen	
With inflated balloon	8F to 10F with 3-ml balloon
	12F to 30F with 5- to 30-ml balloon
Common male sizes	16F to 18F
Common female sizes	12F to 16F

Triple lumen is used for continuous bladder irrigation. Coudé-tip catheter is used for men with an enlarged prostate gland.

PREVENTING URINARY CATHETER INFECTIONS

- Use good hand washing before handling.
- Avoid raising the drainage bag above the bladder.
- Allow urine to drain freely into bag.
- Perform good perineal care on client.
- Secure catheter per procedure.
- Empty drainage bag at least every 8 hours.
- Avoid kinking the tubing.
- Clean spigot thoroughly before and after use.
- Avoid dragging drainage bag on the floor.

*The larger the number, the larger the size.

TIMED URINE TESTS

Quantitative albumin (24 hours) Determines albumin lost in urine as a result of kidney disease, hypertension, or heart failure

Amino acid (24 hours) Determines presence of congenital kidney disease

Amylase (2, 12, and 24 hours) Determines presence of disease of the pancreas

Chloride (24 hours) Determines loss of chloride in cardiac patients on low-salt or no-salt diets

Concentration and dilution Determines presence of diseases of the kidney tubules

Creatinine clearance (12 and 24 hours) Determines the ability of the kidney to clear creatinine

Estriol (24 hours) Measures this hormone in women with high-risk pregnancies caused by diabetes

Glucose tolerance (12 and 24 hours) Determines malfunctions of the liver and pancreas

17-Hydroxycorticosteroid (24 hours) Determines functioning ability of the adrenal cortex

Urinalysis (random times) Determines levels of bacteria, WBC, RBC, pH, specific gravity, protein, and bilirubin

Urine culture (random times) Determines the amount and type of bacteria in the urine

Urine sensitivity (random times) Determines the antibiotics to which the microorganisms will be sensitive or resistant

Urobilinogen (random times) Determines presence of obstruction of the biliary tract

Chapter 15

Reproductive System

For an in-depth study of the reproductive system,
consult the following publications:

AJN/Mosby: *Nursing boards review for the NCLEX-RN examination,* ed 10,
St Louis, 1996, Mosby.

Austrin MG, Austrin HR: *Learning medical terminology,* ed 9, St Louis, 1998,
Mosby.

Lewis SM, Collier IC, Heitkemper MM: *Medical-surgical nursing,* ed 5,
St Louis, 2000, Mosby.

Patton KT, Thibodeau GA: *Handbook for anatomy and physiology,* St Louis,
2000, Mosby.

Potter PA, Perry AG: *Fundamentals of nursing,* ed 5, St Louis, 2001, Mosby.

MALE STRUCTURES

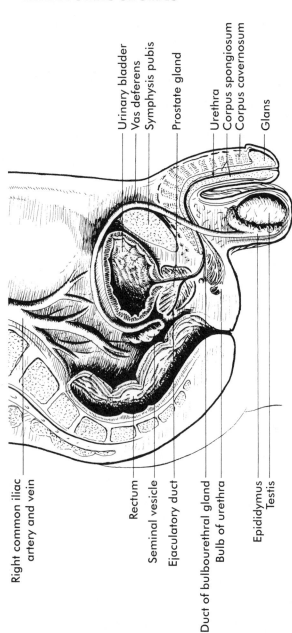

Urinary bladder
Vas deferens
Symphysis pubis

Prostate gland

Urethra
Corpus spongiosum
Corpus cavernosum

Glans

Right common iliac
artery and vein

Rectum
Seminal vesicle
Ejaculatory duct

Duct of bulbourethral gland
Bulb of urethra

Epididymus
Testis

Figure 15-1 Male genitourinary system. (From Austrin MG, Austrin HR: *Learning medical terminology,* ed 9, St Louis, 1998, Mosby.)

FEMALE STRUCTURES

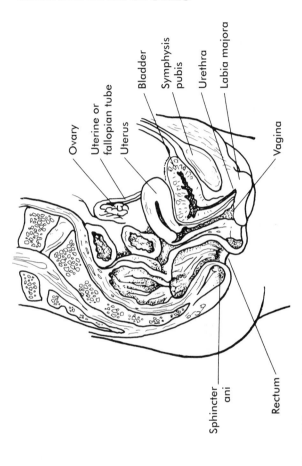

Figure 15-2 Female genitourinary system. (From Austrin MG, Austrin HR: *Learning medical terminology*, ed 9, St Louis, 1998, Mosby.)

ASSESSING SEXUAL HISTORY
Include the following information:

Male
Practice of testicular examinations
Last prostate examination and results
Knowledge of deficit
Concerns or difficulty with sexual activities
Body image concerns
Concerns regarding the effect of treatment on future sexual activities
Attitudes regarding sex

Female
Last menstrual cycle
Onset of menopause
Knowledge deficit
Number of pregnancies, children, and miscarriages
Body image concerns
Practice of breast self-examination
Last mammogram and results
Last Pap smear and pelvic examination and results
Any concerns or difficulty with sexual activities
Concerns regarding the effect of treatment on future sexual activities
Attitudes regarding sex

MEDICATIONS THAT AFFECT SEXUAL PERFORMANCE*

Antidepressants Blurred vision, confusion, and loss of desire

Antihypertensives Loss of desire, weakness

Antiemetics Impotence, restlessness, and insomnia

Cimetidine Impotence, dizziness, headaches, and nausea

Diuretics Dizziness, headaches, and weakness

Oral contraceptives Allow for sexual activity without concern about conception

Ranitidine Impotence, dizziness, headaches, and nausea

Steroids Mood changes, menstrual changes, headaches, and weakness

Tranquilizers Drowsiness, confusion, and decreased sexual desire

*Consult a drug reference book for more information on specific drugs and their side effects.

Common Male Reproductive Disorders

Disorder	Description	Assess for
Hydrocele	Collection of fluid in testes	Pain, swelling
Spermatocele	Cystic mass of the epididymis	Pain, swelling
Varicocele	Dilation of spermatic vein	Pain, swelling
Torsion of spermatic cord	Kinking of cord	Sexual dysfunction
Cancer	Testicular cancer	Enlarged testes, lump
	Penile cancer	Growths, fatigue, weight loss, dysfunction
	Prostate cancer	Urinary dysfunction
Urethritis	Inflammation of urethra	Urgency, frequency, burning with urination
Prostatitis	Inflammation of prostate	Pain, fever, dysuria, urethral drainage
Epididymitis	Inflammation of epididymis	Scrotal pain, edema
Benign prostatic hypertrophy	Enlarged prostate	Dysuria, pain

Common Female Reproductive Disorders

Disorder	Description	Assess for
Uterine prolapse	Displacement of uterus	Dysmenorrhea, backache, pelvic pain
Cystocele	Bladder herniation into vagina	Backache, stress incontinence
Rectocele	Rectum herniation into vagina	Constipation, hemorrhoids
Ovarian cyst	Enlarged ovaries	Menstrual changes, abdominal swelling
Endometriosis	Seeding of endometrial cells into pelvis	Pain, infertility, menstrual changes
Cervical polyps	Benign tumor	Bleeding between periods and with intercourse, increased cervical mucosa
Cancer	Cervical cancer	Spotting, pain
	Uterine cancer	Pain, abdominal fullness, postmenopausal bleeding
	Ovarian cancer	Ascites, fatigue, weight loss, abdominal fullness

Sexually Transmitted Diseases*

Organism	Diseases	Symptoms	Treatment
Bacteria	Gonorrhea, chancroid, granuloma	Purulent discharge	Penicillin
Spirochete	Syphilis	Stage 1: chancre Stage 2: body rash Stage 3: tumors, nerve damage, cardiac damage	Penicillin
Chlamydia	Nongonococcal urethritis, cervicitis, epididymitis, pelvic inflammatory disease	Purulent drainage, fever, chills, pain, and vomiting	Antibiotics
Virus	Herpes, cytomegalovirus (HPV) AIDS	Vesicles Pulmonary infections	Acyclovir Antibiotics, supportive care
Protozoa	Trichomoniasis	Itching, greenish discharge	Vinegar
Yeast	Candidiasis	Itching, white, cheesy discharge	Nystatin, miconazole

*Sexually transmitted diseases are any disorders that can be transmitted from one person to another during sexual contact.

Chapter 16

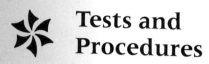

Tests and Procedures

For an in-depth study of tests and procedures,
consult the following publications:

AJN/Mosby: *Nursing boards review for the NCLEX-RN examination,* ed 10,
   St Louis, 1996, Mosby.

Austrin MG, Austrin HR: *Learning medical terminology,* ed 9, St Louis, 1998,
   Mosby.

Lewis SM, Collier IC, Heitkemper MM: *Medical-surgical nursing,* ed 5,
   St Louis, 2000, Mosby.

Myers JL: *Quick medication administration reference,* ed 2, St Louis, 1995,
   Mosby.

Pagana KD, Pagana TJ: *Mosby's diagnostic and laboratory test reference,*
   ed 4, St Louis, 1999, Mosby.

Potter PA, Perry AG: *Fundamentals of nursing,* ed 5, St Louis, 2001, Mosby.

LABORATORY VALUES*
Complete Blood Cell Count

Red blood cells (RBC)	$4.25\text{-}6.1 \times 10$/ml (males)
	$3.6\text{-}5.4 \times 10$/ml (females)
White blood cells (WBC)	$5000\text{-}10,000$/mm^3
Hemoglobin (Hgb)	13-18 g/dl (males)
	12-16 g/dl (females)
Hematocrit (Hct)	45%-54% (males)
	37%-47% (females)

Coagulation

Platelet	150,000-350,000/ml
Prothrombin time (PT)	10-14 sec
Partial thromboplastin time (PTT)	30-45 sec
Thrombin time (TT)	Control $\pm$ 5 sec
Fibrinogen split products (FSP)	Negative reaction at >1:4 dilution
Iron/ferritin (Fe) (deficiency)	0-20 ng/ml
Reticulocyte count	0.5%-1.5% of RBC

*Averages may vary per facility.

Blood Chemistry

Sodium (Na^+)	135-145 mEq/L
Potassium (K^+)	3.5-4.5 mEq/L
Chloride (Cl^-)	98-106 mEq/L
Carbon dioxide (CO_2)	24-32 mEq/L
Blood urea nitrogen (BUN)	7-25 mg/dl
Creatinine (Cr)	0.7-1.3 mg/dl (males)
	0.6-1.2 mg/dl (females)
Glucose	70-110 mg/dl
Calcium (Ca^{++})	8.5-10.5 mg/dl
Magnesium (Mg)	1.3-2.1 mg/dl
Phosphorus	3.0-4.5 mg/dl
Osmolality	275-295 mOsm/kg
Bilirubin	
Direct	0-0.2 mg/dl
Total	0.2-1.0 mg/dl
Indirect is total minus direct	
Amylase	50-150 U/L
Lipase	0-110 U/L
Anion gap	8-16 mEq/L

Urine Electrolytes

Sodium (Na^+)	40-220 mEq/L
Potassium (K^+)	25-125 mEq/L
Chloride (Cl^-)	110-250 mEq/L

ARTERIAL BLOOD GASES

Acid-base balance (pH) Measures hydrogen concentration (7.35-7.45)

Oxygenation (Pao$_2$) Measures partial pressure of dissolved oxygen in the blood (80-100 mm Hg)

Saturation (So$_2$) Measures percentage of oxygen to hemoglobin (95%-98%)

Ventilation (Paco$_2$) Measures partial pressure of carbon dioxide (38-45 mm Hg)

Nursing Interventions

Preparation. Cleanse the area over the artery with an iodine cleaner. Collect an arterial blood gas (ABG) syringe, needle, and heparin.

Collection. An ABG test must be done by a physician, specially trained nurse, or laboratory technician. Keep the client calm.

Post-ABG. The sample will need to go to the laboratory immediately. Some facilities may require an advance call to the laboratory before an ABG test specimen can be sent.

Acid-Base Imbalances

Clinical Manifestations

Acidosis	Alkalosis

Respiratory Manifestations
Causes

Carbonic excess, pneumonia, hyperventilation, obesity

Carbonic deficit, anxiety, fear, hyperventilation, anemia, asthma

Signs and Symptoms

Confusion/CNS depression

Unconsciousness (late sign)

Laboratory Values

pH 7.25 (low)
$Paco_2$ 60 mm Hg (high)
Bicarbonate normal
$Paco_2$ 60 mm Hg (acute)
Pao_2 80 mm Hg (chronic)

pH 7.52 (high)
$Paco_2$ 31 mm Hg (low)
Bicarbonate normal
Pao_2 90 mm Hg (high)

Metabolic Manifestations
Causes

Bicarbonate deficit, ketoacidosis, starvation, shock, diarrhea, renal failure

Bicarbonate excess, Cushing's syndrome, hypokalemia, hypercalcemia, excessive vomiting, diuretics

Signs and Symptoms

Weakness, disorientation, coma

Respiratory depression, tetany, mental dullness

Continued

Acid-Base Imbalances—cont'd

Clinical Manifestations

Acidosis	Alkalosis
Laboratory Values	
pH <7.35	pH >7.45
Urine pH <6	Urine pH >7
$Paco_2$ normal	$Paco_2$ normal
$K^+ >5$	$K^+ <3.5$
Bicarbonate <21 mEq/L	Bicarbonate >28 mEq/L

ELECTROLYTE IMBALANCES
Clinical Manifestations
Hyponatremia (<135 mEq/L)
Signs and Symptoms. Fatigue, abdominal cramps, diarrhea, weakness, hypotension, cool, clammy skin.
Causes. Overhydration, kidney disease, diarrhea.

Hypernatremia (>145 mEq/L)
Signs and Symptoms. Thirst, dry, sticky mucous membranes, dry tongue and skin, flushed skin, increased body temperature.
Causes. Dehydration, starvation, syndrome of inappropriate antidiuretic hormone secretion (SIADH).

Hypokalemia (<3.5 mEq/L)
Signs and Symptoms. Weakness, fatigue, anorexia, abdominal distention, arrhythmias, decreased bowel sounds.
Causes. Diarrhea, diuretics, alkalosis, polyuria.

Hyperkalemia (>5 mEq/L)
Signs and Symptoms. Anxiety, arrhythmias, increased bowel sounds.
Causes. Burns, renal failure, dehydration, acidosis.

Hypocalcemia (<8.3 mEq/L)
Signs and Symptoms. Abdominal cramps, tingling, muscle spasms, convulsions; assess magnesium level.
Causes. Parathyroid dysfunction, vitamin D deficiency, pancreatitis.

Hypercalcemia (>10 mEq/L)
Signs and Symptoms. Deep bone pain, nausea, vomiting, constipation; assess magnesium level.
Causes. Parathyroid tumor, bone cancer/metastasis, osteoporosis.

Hypomagnesemia (<1.3 mEq/L)

Signs and Symptoms. Tremors, muscle cramps, tachycardia, hypertension, confusion; assess calcium level.

Causes. Parathyroid dysfunction, cancer, chemotherapy, polyuria.

Hypermagnesemia (>2.5mEq/L)

Signs and Symptoms. Lethargy, respiratory difficulty, coma; assess calcium level.

Causes. Parathyroid dysfunction, renal failure.

FLUID VOLUME IMBALANCES
Fluid Volume Deficit (Hypovolemia)

Signs and Symptoms. Hypotension, weight loss, decreased tearing or saliva, dry skin or mouth, oliguria, increased pulse or respirations, increased specific gravity of urine, increased serum sodium levels.

Causes. Dehydration, insufficient fluid intake, diuretics, sweating or polyuria, excessive tube feedings leading to diarrhea.

Fluid Volume Excess (Hypervolemia)

Signs and Symptoms. Edema, puffy face or eyelids, ascites, rales or wheezes in lungs, bounding pulse, hypertension, sudden weight gain, decreased serum sodium levels.

Causes. Overhydration, renal failure, congestive heart failure.

Common Fluid Volumes*

Small glass of water: 200 ml

Small bowl of soup: 180 ml

Water pitcher: 1 liter

Ice cream: 120 ml

Juice: 120 ml

Teapot: 240 ml

Gelatin: 120 ml

Medium cup: 30 ml

Common IV Solutions

Normal saline–0.9% saline (NS)

5% Dextrose in water (D_5W)

5% Dextrose in 0.9% saline (D_5NS)

5% Dextrose in 0.45% saline (D_5 ½NS)

Lactated Ringer's (NaCl, K^+, Ca^{++}, lactic acid)

*Volumes may vary per institution.

Drugs Affecting Hemostasis

Medication	Drug Class	Peak Time	Duration	Half-Life
Alteplase	Thrombolytic	5-10 min	2-3 hr	5 min
Anistreplase	Thrombolytic	45 min	4-6 hr	70-120 min
Aspirin	Antiplatelet	15 min-2 hr	4-6 hr	15-30 min
Dalteparin	Anticoagulant	3-5 hr	12 hr	3.5 hr
Dipyridamole	Antiplatelet	75 min (PO)	3-4 hr	10 hr
		6.5 min (IV)	30 min	10 hr
Enoxaparin	Anticoagulant	3-5 hr	12 hr	4.5 hr
Heparin	Anticoagulant	2-4 hr (SQ)	8-12 hr	1-2 hr
		5-10 min (IM)	2-6 hr	1-2 hr
Ibuprofen	NSAID/antiplatelet	1-2 hr	4-6 hr	1.8-2 hr

Ketorolac	NSAID/antiplatelet	30-60 min (PO)	4-6 hr	2-8 hr
		30-90 min (IM)	4-8 hr	5-6 hr
Pentoxifylline	Antiplatelet	1-4 hr	Unknown	0.8-1.6 hr
Plavix	Antiplatelet	1 hr	Unknown	8 hr
Reteplase	Thrombolytic	5-10 min	Unknown	13-16 min
Streptokinase	Thrombolytic	30-60 min	4-12 hr	23 min
Sulfinpyrazone	Antiplatelet	1-2 hr	4-6 hr	4 hr
Ticlopidine	Antiplatelet	2 hr	14-21 days	12.6 hr single dose
				4-5 days multidose
Urokinase	Thrombolytic	End of infusion	12 hr	20 min
Warfarin	Anticoagulant	0.5-3 days	2-5 days	0.5-3 days

Data from *Drug Facts & Comparisons*, St. Louis, 2002, Facts & Comparisons; Physicians' desk reference, ed 54, Montvale, NJ, 2000, Medical Economics.

DIAGNOSTIC TESTS

Angiography Records cardiac pressures, function, and output (Client may need special post-procedure vital signs taken.)

Antinuclear antibody (ANA) A group of antibodies used to diagnose lupus (SLE)

Arterial blood gases Measurements of arterial blood pH, Po_2, $Paco_2$, and bicarbonate (Blood sample needs to be kept on ice.)

Arteriography Radiographic examination with injections of dye used to locate occlusions (Client may need special postprocedure vital signs taken.)

Arthrography Radiographic examination of the bones

Arthroscopy Procedure that allows examination of the joint

Barium study Radiographic examination to locate polyps, tumors, or other colon problems (Barium needs to be removed after procedure.)

Barium swallow Detects esophageal narrowing, varices, strictures, or tumors (Barium needs to be removed after procedure.)

Biopsy Removal of specific tissue (Assess client for pain after procedure.)

Blood tests See section on laboratory values for normal values

Bone densitometry Test to determine bone mineral content and density; used to diagnose osteoporosis

Bone marrow biopsy Examination of a piece of tissue from bone marrow (Assess client for pain after procedure.)

Bone scan Radioisotope used to locate tumors or other bone disorders (Client must be able to lie flat.)

Brain scan Radioisotope used to locate tumors, strokes, or seizure disorders (Client must be able to lie flat.)

Bronchoscopy Inspection of the larynx, trachea, and bronchi with flexible scope (Client may need sedation.)

Cardiac catheterization Uses dye to visualize the heart's arteries (Client may need special post-procedure vital signs taken.)

Chest x-ray (radiograph) Used to look for pneumonia, cancer, and other diseases of the lung

Cholangiography Radiographic examination of the biliary ducts

Cholecystography Radiographic examination of the gallbladder

Colonoscopy Uses flexible scope to view colon (Client may need to be sedated.)

Colposcopy Examination of the cervix and vagina

Computed tomography (CT) scan Three-dimensional radiography (Client must be able to lie flat.)

Culdoscopy Flexible tube used to view pelvic organs

Culture and sensitivity Determines source and type of bacteria

Cystoscopy Direct visualization of bladder with cystoscope

Dilatation and curettage Dilatation of the cervix followed by endometrial cleansing (done in surgery)

Doppler Ultrasound used to show venous or arterial patency

Echocardiography Ultrasound that records structure and functions of the heart

Electrocardiography Records electrical impulses generated by the heart

Electroencephalography Records electrical activity of the brain (Client should be resting.)

Electromyography Records electrical activity of the muscles

Endoscopy Inspection of upper GI tract with flexible scope (Client may need to be sedated.)

Endoscopic retrograde cholangiopancreatography (ERCP) Radiographic examination of the gallbladder and pancreas

Exercise stress test Recording of the heart rate, activity, and blood pressure while the body is at work

Fluoroscopy Radiographic examination with picture displayed on television monitor

GI series Radiographic examination using barium to locate ulcers (Barium must be removed after procedure.)

Glucose tolerance test (GTT) To determine ability to tolerate an oral glucose load; used to establish diabetes

Hemoccult Detects blood in stool, emesis, and elsewhere

Holter monitor Checks and records irregular heart rates and rhythms (generally over a 24-hour period)

Intravenous pyelography (IVP) Radiographic examination of the kidneys after dye injection

KUB Radiographic examination of the kidneys, ureter, and bladder

Laparoscopy Abdominal examination with a flexible scope

Lumbar puncture Sampling of spinal fluid, often called a spinal tap (can be done bedside)

Magnetic resonance imaging (MRI) Three-dimensional radiograph similar to CT scan

Mammography Radiographic examination of the breast

Myelography Injection of dye into subarachnoid space to view brain and spinal cord

Oximetry Method to monitor arterial blood saturation

Pap smear Detects cervical cancer

Proctoscopy Inspection of lower colon with flexible scope (Client may need to be sedated.)

Pulmonary function test (PFT) Measures lung capacity and volume to detect problems

Pyelography Radiographic examination of kidneys

Sigmoidoscopy Inspection of lower colon with flexible scope (Client may need to be sedated.)

Small bowel follow-through (SBFT) Done in addition to a GI series

Spinal tap See Lumbar puncture

Thallium Radionuclear dye used to assess heart functions

Titer A blood test to determine the presence of antibodies

Tuberculin skin test Test for tuberculosis using tuberculin purified protein derivative (PPD)

Ultrasound Reflection of sound waves

Urine tests See Chapter 14

Venography Radiographic examination used to locate a thrombus in a vein

Chapter 17

Surgical Nursing Care

For an in-depth study of surgical nursing care,
consult the following publications:

Beare PG, Myers JL: *Adult health nursing,* ed 3, St Louis, 1998, Mosby.
Lewis SM, Collier IC, Heitkemper MM: *Medical-surgical nursing,* ed 5,
    St Louis, 2000, Mosby.
Meeker MH: *Alexander's care of the patient in surgery,* ed 10, St Louis,
    1995, Mosby.
Potter PA, Perry AG: *Fundamentals of nursing,* ed 5, St Louis, 2001, Mosby.

NURSING CARE BEFORE SURGERY

Teaching

Include the following information:

Smoking or drinking restrictions before surgery

Dietary or fluid restrictions before surgery

Review of surgical procedure

Postoperative deep breathing, positioning, and range of motion exercises

Postoperative pain and pain relief measures available

Postoperative activity or dietary restrictions

Postoperative dressing procedures

Review of drains, nasogastric, catheter, and IV lines that may be inserted during surgery

History

Include the following information:

Chief complaint or reason for surgery

Prior surgeries and responses or impressions

Drug allergies

Physical limitations such as vision or hearing problems, limps, or paralysis

History of smoking and drinking (last drink or food intake)

Medications and the last time taken

Nonprescription or recreational drug use and when taken last

History of strokes, heart attacks, seizures, diabetes, and thyroid or adrenal diseases

Concerns, questions, or special requests

Significant others and where they can be reached after surgery

Checklist
Include the following information:
Signed consent form in the front of the chart
List of clothes and valuables and their placement in a
   safe place
Record of vital signs and last time voided
List of prostheses such as dentures and limbs re-
   moved
List of preoperative medications and when adminis-
   tered
Review of preoperative laboratory values and tests
Preoperative surgical scrubbing (Figures 17-1 and
   17-2)

Review of Body Systems
Note any problems, including the following:
Cardiac Arrhythmia, edema, cyanosis, chest pain,
   hypertension, murmur, heart rate, blood pressure
Respiratory Cough, shortness of breath, dyspnea,
   wheezing, orthopnea, orthostasis, diminished
   sounds, rate, depth
Neurologic Headaches, dizziness, ringing in ears,
   gait, reflexes, muscle strength, emotions
Gastrointestinal Nausea, vomiting, weight gain or
   loss, ulcers, Crohn's disease or ulcerative colitis,
   devices
Genitourinary Urgency, frequency, retention,
   urinary tract infections, need for Foley catheter
   or other devices
Skin Bruising, open sores, rashes, signs of infection,
   general condition

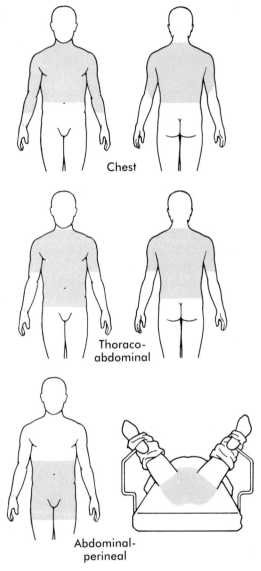

Chest

Thoraco-
abdominal

Abdominal-
perineal

Figure 17-1 Surgical skin preparations.

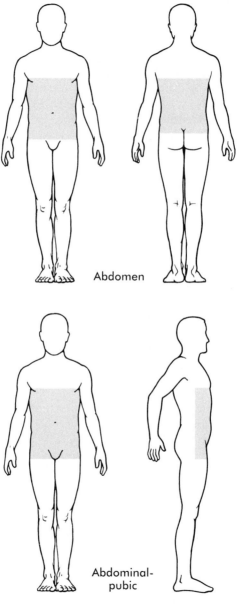

Abdomen

Abdominal-pubic

Figure 17-2 Surgical skin preparations.

NURSING CARE AFTER SURGERY
Objectives
Provide a safe environment for the client.
Monitor the client's condition.
Recognize potential complications.
Prevent complications.

Information Needed*
Type of surgery and anesthetic
Findings and results of the surgery
Any complications during the surgery
Transfusions given during surgery
Current respiratory condition of the client
Current cardiac and circulatory condition of the client
Types and number of incisions, drains, tubes, and IV lines
Current vital signs and when they need to be taken next
Current laboratory values and when specimens need to be drawn next
Dressing location, condition, and changes (the first change is generally done by the surgeon)
Neurologic status and need for future neurologic checks
Time, frequency, and route of administration of pain medications
Additional postoperative orders
Notify any family or significant others waiting for the client

*Can be found in the chart.

CARE OF BODY SYSTEMS
AFTER SURGERY
Cardiac
Possibility of hemorrhage, shock, embolism, thrombosis.

Monitor blood pressure, heart rate, rhythm, quality.

Check for Homans' sign, leg tenderness, leg edema.

Check capillary refill, hemorrhage, shock, pedal pulses.

Pulmonary
Possibility of obstruction, atelectasis, pneumonia.

Turn client every 1 to 2 hours unless contraindicated.

Have client cough and deep breathe using pillows to splint incisions every 1 to 2 hours.

Assess lungs for rales, rhonchi, or wheezes.

Check oxygen saturation per policy protocol and/or with each check of vital signs.

Perform oral or deep suction as needed.

Have client use incentive spirometer as ordered every 1 to 2 hours.

Use humidification to ease breathing, and chest therapy if ordered.

Ensure adequate hydration to help thin secretions and postural drainage to drain secretions.

Assess for adequate pain relief to help breathing.

Neurologic
Perform neurologic and reflex checks as needed.

Assess orientation, level of consciousness, and pain control as needed.

Assess for restlessness, fatigue, and anxiety.

Explain the need for the procedures to the client.

Genitourinary

Assess for adequate fluid intake and output and for bladder distention.

Assess the need for and care of Foley catheter or need for straight catheterization.

Gastrointestinal

Assess bowel sounds for possible ileus (indicated by no sounds).

Assess for nausea, vomiting, distended abdomen, and gas pains.

Skin

Assess wound for drainage and signs of infection.

Assess for skin breakdown.

TYPES OF DRESSINGS

Name	Uses
Absorbent	Drains wound (increases evaporation)
Antiseptic	Prevents infection
Dry	With wound with little or no drainage
Hot/moist	Promotes wound healing by second or third intention; increases blood supply to wound
Occlusive	Prevents invasion of bacteria
Protective	Protects wound from injury
Wet to damp	Dressing removed before wound drys
Wet to dry	With open wound that has necrotic tissue; wounds with greatest drainage
Wet to wet	With wound that needs to be kept very moist

COMMON SURGICAL PROCEDURES*

Anastomosis Creation of a passage between two vessels

Angiectomy/angioplasty Removal/repair of a vessel

Aortotomy Incision into the aorta

Arteriectomy/arterioplasty Removal/repair of an artery

Arthrectomy/arthroplasty Removal/repair of a joint

Atriotomy Incision into an atrium of the heart

Biopsy Incision to remove a tissue sample

Bronchotomy/bronchoplasty Incision into repair of bronchus

Cholecystectomy Removal of the gallbladder

Choledochectomy Removal of a portion of the common bile duct

Colectomy Partial removal of the colon

Coronary artery bypass graft (CABG) A large vein from the body is removed and sutured to either side of an obstructed coronary artery

Craniectomy/cranioplasty Removal/repair of a portion of the skull

Cystectomy/cystoplasty Removal/repair of the bladder

Dermabrasion Surgical removal of epidermis or a portion of the dermis

Embolization Suturing or sealing of a vessel

Esophagectomy/esophagoplasty Removal/repair of the esophagus

Fasciectomy/fascioplasty Removal/repair of the fascia

Gastrectomy/gastroplasty Removal/repair of the stomach

---

*Refer to sections on prefixes and suffixes to build surgical vocabulary.

Graft Surgical replacement of tissue, skin, or muscle

Hysterectomy Removal of the uterus

Laminectomy Removal of the posterior arch of a vertebra

Laryngectomy/laryngoplasty Removal/repair of the larynx

Lymphangiectomy/lymphangioplasty Removal/repair of a lymph vessel

Mastectomy/mastopexy Removal/reduction of a breast

Myectomy/myoplasty Removal/repair of a muscle

Nephrectomy Removal of a kidney

Oophorectomy/oophoroplasty Removal/repair of an ovary

Orchiectomy/orchioplasty Removal/repair of a testicle

Osteoclasis Reconstruction of a fractured bone

Percutaneous transluminal coronary angioplasty (PTCA) A balloon procedure used to push an obstruction against a vessel wall to allow blood to flow through

Pericardiectomy Removal of the pericardium

Phlebectomy/phleboplasty Removal/repair of a vein

Pneumonectomy Removal of a lung

Radical mastectomy Removal of a breast, pectorals, lymph nodes, and skin

Rhinoplasty Plastic repair of the nose

Splenotomy/splenorrhapy Incision into/repair of the spleen

Thoracoplasty Removal of a rib to allow collapse of the lungs

Valvulotomy/valvuloplasty Incision into/repair of a valve

RED BLOOD CELL TRANSFUSIONS

Typing Selecting the ABO blood type and Rh antigen factor of a person's blood (other antigens can also affect transfusion compatibility)

Cross-matching Mixing the recipient's serum with the donor's red blood cells in a saline solution; if no agglutination occurs, the blood may be safely given

Blood Type	Can Generally Donate to	Can Generally Receive From
A−	A−, A+	A−, O−
B−	B−, B+	B−, O−
AB−	AB−, AB+	AB−, A−, B−, O−
A+	A+	A+, A−, O+, O−
B+	B+	B+, B−, O+, O−
AB+	AB+	All blood types
O−	All blood types	O−
O+	O+, A+, B+, AB+	O+, O−

Before Administering Blood to a Client

Check facility's policy on infusing blood products.

Check the client's ID band for proper identification.

Check the client's blood type and Rh antigen.

Get the blood from blood bank only when ready to infuse.

Compare the client's blood type with the type of blood to be infused.

Two people should check and cosign blood.

Start infusion of blood with normal saline solution.

Administer blood at a slower rate for the first 15 minutes. Blood should be infused within 4 hours.

Use appropriate blood tubing and needles (may vary per facility).

Document action on appropriate flow sheets (may vary per facility).

Instruct client to report *any* discomfort (blood re-
    actions).
Special vital signs are needed (may vary per facility).
Some facilities may medicate the client with acet-
    aminophen or diphenhydramine (Benadryl) be-
    fore infusion.

Blood Reactions

Possible reactions include difficulty breathing, wheezing, tachypnea, fever, tachycardia, change in blood
pressure, chest pain, disorientation, rash, or hives. *If a
reaction begins, stop the infusion.* Begin a normal saline
flush to keep the IV line open and administer prescribed antihistamines. Notify a physician, recheck
blood, retype, and cross-match. *Do not* discard the
blood—the laboratory may want to analyze it for the
cause of the reaction. The physician may require a
urine sample from the client.

BLOOD TRANSFUSION ALTERNATIVES

Considerations for clients who may refuse blood transfusions based on cultural or religious reasons.

Volume Expanders

Crystalloid—Ringer's lactate, normal saline, hypertonic saline
Colloids—Dextran, gelatin, hetastarch
Perfluorochemicals—Fluosol DA-20

Hemostatic Agents for Bleeding/Clotting Problems

Topical—Avitene, Gelfoam, Oxycel, Surgicel
Injectable—Desmopressin, tranexamic acid,
   ϵ-aminocaproic acid, vitamin K

Techniques and Agents for Managing Anemia

Oxygen support
Maintain intravascular volume
Nutritional support
Iron
Dextran (Imferon)
Folic acid
Vitamin B_{12}
Erythropoietin
Granulocyte colony-stimulating factor (GCSF)
Perfluorocarbon solutions

Techniques to Limit Blood Loss During Surgery

Hypotensive anesthesia
Induced hypothermia
Intraoperative blood salvage
Intraoperative or hypervolemia hemodilution
Reduce blood flow to skin
Mechanical occlusion of bleeding vessels
Meticulous hemostasis

Techniques That Can Limit Blood Sampling
Transcutaneous pulse oximeter
Pulse oximeter
Pediatric microsampling
Planning ahead with multiple tests per sample

Techniques to Locate and Arrest Internal Bleeding
Electrocautery
Laser surgery
Argon beam coagulator
Endoscope
Gamma knife radiosurgery
Embolization

Chapter 18

 Client Safety

For an in-depth study of client safety, consult
the following publications:

Lueckenotte AB: *Pocket guide to gerontologic assessment,* ed 3, St Louis, 1998, Mosby.
Potter PA, Perry AG: *Fundamentals of nursing,* ed 5, St Louis, 2001, Mosby.

ADMISSION SAFETY

When a client is admitted to the hospital or nursing home, it is important that the client is aware of all equipment located in his or her room. This can prevent accidents and make the hospital or nursing home stay safer. Point out the following items on admission: call light or bell, room lights, bathroom, bathroom lights, nurses' station, side rails, and room number.

Make sure that all equipment is working properly.

ONGOING SAFETY

To ensure ongoing safety, take the following precautions:

Clear the client's room of excess debris.

No furniture should be blocking the doorway to the client's room.

Immediately clean up any water or other liquid spills on the floor.

Do not leave needles or other sharp items near the client.

Remove unmarked bottles and syringes from client's room.

Label all IV and central lines and nasogastric, gastrostomy, and jejunostomy tubes.

Check all electrical equipment for proper functioning and condition.

Double check all medications before giving them to the client, using the six client rights.

Double check the client ID bracelet before giving medications, performing any procedures, and transferring the client to another department for tests, another unit, surgery, or therapy appointments.

SPECIAL CLIENT SITUATIONS

Hospitalized clients with the following problems may require additional safety measures:

Alcohol Withdrawal

Signs and Symptoms. Confusion, sweating, pallor, palpitations, hypotension, seizures, coma. Protocols may vary by facility.

Withdrawal protocols may include seizure precautions, keeping the side rails up and padded, taking vital signs frequently (every 30 to 60 minutes or per hospital protocol), and close observation. Provide a safe environment. Perform neurologic, memory, or orientation checks. Document any withdrawal activity and actions taken.

Bleeding/Hemorrhage

Locate the source of the bleeding. Apply direct pressure with a clean drape. Call for assistance but stay with the client. Assess for early signs of shock such as changes in sensorium and later signs of shock such as hypotension, pale skin, and a rapid, weak pulse.

Prevention. Closely supervise confused or heavily medicated clients and clients just returning from surgery. Make sure surgical dressings are secure. Encourage clients to call for assistance if bleeding begins. Document any bleeding and actions taken.

Choking

Follow standard Heimlich maneuver guidelines.

Prevention. Closely supervise confused or heavily medicated clients. Make sure clients are sitting up or are placed in high Fowler's position when eating. Encourage the use of the call lights. Assess the client's ability to chew and swallow. Order a diet appropriate to the client's eating ability. Document any choking situations and actions taken.

Drug Reactions

Assess for difficulty breathing, wheezing, tearing, palpitations, skin rash, pruritus, nausea or vomiting, rhinitis, diarrhea, and a change in mood or mental status. *These are general drug reactions, not the side effects of specific drugs. Immediately report all drug reactions.*

Prevention. Closely supervise confused or heavily medicated clients, or those clients who are taking medications for the first time. Encourage the use of the call lights should any of the signs of a drug reaction occur. *Know your client's drug allergies.* Document all drug reactions and actions taken.

THE CONFUSED CLIENT

Assess for the source of the confusion. Possible sources include age, medications, disease, and infection. The confused client may be at risk for falls.

Falls

Assess for the client's ability to ambulate, environment, mental status, medications.

Prevention. Closely supervise confused or heavily medicated clients, encourage the use of call lights or the use of night lights, raise side rails, post sign alerting others of the possibility of falls, lock wheelchair, use gait belts, encourage client to use grab bars or side rails, avoid water/liquid spills, and use nonskid footwear.

Falls Assessment Checklist

One or more of the following items can place a person at risk for falls:

_____ Over 70 years old
_____ Hearing or visual loss
_____ Disoriented/confused
_____ History of falls
_____ Does not speak or understand English
_____ Diuretic use
_____ Electrolyte imbalance
_____ Cardiac disease
_____ Recent MI
_____ Uncontrolled diabetes

_____ Weak
_____ Urinary frequency
_____ Agitated
_____ Uses cane or walker
_____ Psychotropic drug use
_____ Cardiac drug use
_____ Hypotensive
_____ Neurologic disease
_____ Peripheral vascular disease
_____ Recent CVA

Restraints
When to Use
- To prevent injury
- To restrict movement
- To immobilize a body part
- To prevent harm to self or others

  Restraints should be used only when all other methods of keeping a client safe have been tried.

Types of Restraints
Jackets/vests, belts, mittens, wrist or ankle, crib net, elbow.

Guidelines
- Obtain physician's order and follow facility protocol.
- Explain purpose to client; check circulation every 30 minutes.
- Release temporarily (once per hour).
- Provide range of motion.
- Document need and examination schedule.
- Report problems and tolerance; provide emotional support.

  Never secure restraints to the side rails or the nonstationary portion of the main frame of the bed.

Complications
- Skin breakdown (pad bony areas)
- Nerve damage (do not overtighten, release often)
- Circulatory impairment (check for problems often, provide range of motion)
- Death (from inadequate or improper use)

Prevention

- Keep the side rails up when you are not with the client.
- Monitor vital signs and the client's drug doses and levels.
- Monitor the client's electrolytes and neurologic status.
- Reorient client to place and time as needed.
- Place call light in easy reach.
- Attend closely to personal care needs.
- Encourage family, friends, and clergy to visit often.

Comparison of Delirium and Dementia

Feature	Delirium	Dementia
Onset	Rapid, often at night	Usually insidious
Duration	Hours to weeks	Months to years
Course	Fluctuates over 24 hr	Relatively stable
	Worse at night	
	Lucid intervals	
Awareness	Always impaired	Usually normal
Alertness	Fluctuates	Usually normal
Orientation	Impaired; often will mistake people or places	May be intact
		May confabulate

Memory	Recent and immediate memory impaired	Recent and remote memory impaired
Thinking	Slow, accelerated, or dreamlike	Poor in abstraction Impoverished
Perception	Often misperceptions	Becomes absent
Sleep cycle	Disrupted at night Drowsiness during day	Fragmented sleep
Physical	Often sick	Often well at first

COMMON PSYCHIATRIC DISORDERS

Alcoholic psychosis A confused, disoriented state after intoxication

Anorexia nervosa An eating disorder. Loss of appetite for food not explainable by disease

Anxiety disorder No mechanisms to block varying degrees of anxiety

Bulimia Disorder in which vomiting is self-induced after eating large amounts of food

Conversion disorder Sensory or motor impairment in the absence of organic cause

Depression Feeling of hopelessness or sadness or loss of interest

Dissociative disorder Person escapes stress through memory or identity changes

Korsakoff's syndrome Delirium/hallucinations often caused by chronic alcohol use

Mania Characterized by a state of extreme excitement

Manic-depressive Mood swing of very high to very low

Paranoia Delusions of persecution or of grandeur

Personality disorder Repetitive, irresponsible, and manipulative behaviors

Phobia A morbid fear or anxiety about an item or a place

Psychosis Loss of reality

Psychosomatic Person is limited in coping skills, which produces physical effects

Schizophrenia Profoundly withdrawn from reality, often with bizarre behaviors

COMMON PSYCHIATRIC TESTS

Beck Depression Inventory Self-report measure of feelings and attitudes

Brief Psychiatric Rating Scale Standardized rating scale for person over 18 years old

Rorschach Test Ten ink blots used to analyze thought processes

Thematic Apperception Test Unstructured set of pictures where the client makes up stories to uncover conflict or to reveal needs

Wechsler Adult Intelligence Scale Verbal and cognitive test

TREATMENT METHODS

Antipsychotic drugs Antipsychotics and tranquilizers

Antidepressant drugs Tricyclics and monoamine oxidase (MAO) inhibitors

Antianxiety drugs Minor tranquilizers or propanediols and benzodiazepines

Behavior modification Rewards given to modify behavior

Behavior therapy Aversion therapy to modify behavior

Cognitive therapy Patient examines his or her own beliefs and attitudes

Electroconvulsive therapy Shock therapy given to the brain to induce a seizure

Insulin therapy To treat schizophrenics, places client in coma

Prefrontal lobotomy Frontal lobes of the brain are separated

Psychoanalytic therapy Therapy to gain insight into the origins of the condition

Psychotherapies Group therapy of psychiatric disorders

EMERGENCIES

Fire Safety

RACE—**R**escue clients, **A**lert others/pull **A**larm, **C**ontain fire, **E**xtinguish fire. Know the facility's emergency telephone number. Know your location. Speak clearly. Know the facility's fire drill and evacuation plan. Close windows and doors. Turn off oxygen supply. All extinguishers are labeled A, B, C, or D according to the types of fires they are meant to extinguish. Some extinguishers can be used for more than one type of fire and will be labeled with more than one letter. The types of fires the letters correspond to are:

A: Paper or wood
B: Liquid or gas
C: Electrical
D: Combustible metal

Any of the following emergencies may require CPR.

Heart Attack

Signs and Symptoms. Chest pain; shortness of breath; dyspnea; a squeezing, crushing, or heavy feeling in the chest; lightheadedness; pain in left arm or in the jaw; and nausea.

Intervention. Calm the client and turn on the call light. Begin oxygen at 2 liters if nearby. Remain calm and stay with the client until help arrives. Document symptoms and actions taken.

Pulmonary Embolism

Signs and Symptoms. Chest pain, shortness of breath, dyspnea, cyanosis, and possible death.

Causes. Immobility, deep vein thrombosis.

Intervention. Calm client and turn on the call light. Begin oxygen at 2 liters if nearby. Remain calm and stay with the client until help arrives. Document symptoms and actions taken.

Prevention. Elevate legs, use antiembolism stockings, dorsiflexion of foot, perform range of motion exercises, check Homans' sign, perform coughing and deep breathing exercise, and administer low dosages of heparin as prescribed while client is hospitalized. Do not massage lower legs.

Cardiac Arrest

Remain calm and turn on the call light. Begin CPR (follow standard guidelines) until more experienced staff arrives and takes over. Clear furniture from the room and ask family to move to waiting area. (Some facilities will allow family to watch CPR activity.)

Seizures
Signs and Symptoms
Grand mal Total body stiffness, staring, jerking muscles

Petit mal Daydreaming, staring

Causes. Neurologic disease, cancer, head injury, fever, or pregnancy-induced hypertension.

Interventions. Remain calm and turn on the call light. Ensure the client's safety, lower the bed, and raise side rails. Stay with the client, time the seizure, and make sure the client does not hit his or her head. Document seizure activity and actions taken.

Shock
Signs and Symptoms
Mild/early Warm, flushed skin, changes in orientation, widening pulse pressure

Moderate/mild Cool, clammy, pale skin, hypotension, narrowing pulse pressure, sweating, pallor, rapid pulse, decrease in urinary output

Severe/late All the symptoms of moderate/mild shock plus irregular pulse, oliguria, shallow, rapid breathing, obtunded, or comatose

Causes. Hemorrhage, infection, or hypovolemia.

Intervention. Monitor vital signs, assess orientation, and keep the client warm. Record all symptoms and vital signs.

Chapter 19

 # Care of the Dying

For an in-depth study of death and dying, bereavement,
and cultural and religious rituals, consult the
following publications:

Elkin MK, Perry AG, Potter PA: *Nursing intervention and clinical skills,* ed 2,
    St Louis, 2000, Mosby.
Giger JN, Davidhizar RE: *Transcultural nursing: assessment and interven-
    tion,* ed 3, St Louis, 1999, Mosby.
Husted GL, Husted JH: *Ethical decision making in nursing,* ed 2, St Louis,
    1995, Mosby.
Kübler-Ross E: *On death and dying,* New York, 1969, Collier Books.
Kübler-Ross E: *Questions and answers on death and dying,* New York, 1974,
    Collier Books.

STAGES OF DYING AND GRIEF
Denial
- Client or family may refuse to accept the situation.
- Client or family may not believe the diagnosis.
- Client or family may be seeking second and third opinions.
- Client or family may claim that the tests were wrong.
- Client or family may claim that the tests were mixed up with those of someone else.
- Client may sleep more or be overly talkative or cheerful.

Anger
- Client or family may be hostile.
- Client or family may have excessive demands.
- Client may be withdrawn, cold, or unemotional.
- Feelings may include envy, resentment, or rage.
- Client may be angry at family for being well.
- Client may be uncooperative or manipulative.
- **This may be the time that clients are the hardest to care for but the time when they need us the most!**

Bargaining
- Client or family may promise to improve or change habits such as quit smoking, eat less, exercise more.
- Bargaining may be intertwined with feelings of guilt.
- Bargains are often with the physicians or with God.

Depression
- Client or family may speak of the upcoming loss.
- Client or family may cry or weep often.
- Client or family may want to be alone.

Acceptance
- Client may exhibit a decreased interest in the surroundings.
- Client may not want visitors during this time.
- Do not confuse acceptance with depression.
- There seems to be a calmness or peace about the client.

INTERACTING WITH THE DYING CLIENT AND THE FAMILY

Interventions should be based on the stage of dying and grief.

Denial

This stage is used as a coping or protective function and should not be viewed as a bad quality. It can be a time when a client or family can gather their thoughts, feelings, and strengths.

You should:

- Listen, listen, listen (remember, they may talk a lot).
- Get a sense of what they are worried about.
- Be honest with communications.
- Not give the client false hope.
- Not argue with the client or family.

Anger

This is often directed at caregivers; ensure that caregivers will not stop caring.

You should:

- Not take anger personally.
- Help family to not take anger personally.
- Visit the client often and answer call lights promptly.
- Assist the family with much-needed breaks.

Bargaining

Because many of the bargains may be with a divine power, the period may pass unnoticed.

You should:

- Offer frequent chances for the client or family to talk.
- Offer visits from clergy or other supports.

Depression

Some clients or families may not have a good outlet for their depression.

You should:

- Not force cheerful or important conversation.
- Allow the client or family to voice concerns.
- Offer visits from clergy.
- Offer cultural or religious supports.

Acceptance

Client may want to be alone and families may feel rejected.

You should:

- Encourage family to come often but for brief visits.
- Offer visits from clergy.
- Offer cultural or religious supports.

NURSING INTERVENTIONS WITH IMPENDING DEATH
Personal Care
- Good mouth care: keep mouth moist; do not use lemon swabs.
- Skin care: use lotions, massage, good lip care.
- Artificial tears, if eyes are open.
- Adequate pain control with medications, massage, positioning.
- Suctioning if there are increased secretions, to ease breathing.
- Clean and straighten linens often.
- Change position of client as needed to promote comfort.
- Provide adequate hydration.

Recognize Special Needs
- Encourage visits by clergy.
- Assess for the need for Last Rites, Holy Communion.
- Allow for religious music, holy books, and other supports.
- Allow time for the family or friends to pray.
- Encourage cultural or religious rituals or practices.

Preparing the Family

- Describe the physical changes that may be taking place as death approaches.
- Allow the family as much time as possible with the dying client.
- Offer the family opportunities for cultural or religious rituals.
- Keep family updated as to the time of approaching death.
- Be honest when telling the family about the impending death.
- Allow for sleep and hygiene needs of the family or friends.
- Allow family or friends time to voice fears or concerns.
- Allow the family time for questions.
- Allow the family time for tears.

RELIGIOUS DEATH RITUALS

Buddhism Belief in reincarnation; Last Rites and chanting at the bedside are encouraged.

Confucianism Belief in reincarnation; burning incense and flowers are laid at the bedside to assist the spirit on its journey.

Eastern and Russian Orthodox Last Rites must be conducted while the patient is still conscious.

Hindu Patient may wish to be placed on the floor to be closer to the earth in death. Family is encouraged to wash and prepare the body. The *Bhagavadgita,* and the holy book, is read, chapters 2, 8, and 25.

Jehovah's Witness There are no special death rites; however, church elders may assist the family with final arrangements.

Judaism (Conservative/Orthodox) The body is washed by the burial society and wrapped in white linen. No embalming or flowers are used. A cantor will assist the rabbi in the funeral. Burial should be done within 24 hours and should not be done on the Sabbath.

Judaism (Reform/Liberal) No restrictions on the time or day of removal or burial.

Lutheran May accept Holy Communion, and Last Rites are optional.

Methodist and Baptist May wish to invite religious clergy to be near at the time of death.

Mormon Anointing of the sick and Communion are encouraged. Church elder may assist the family with arrangements. The body is washed by the relief society. If the person has been "through the temple," the person is dressed in white with a green apron.

Muslim Chapter 36 of the *Qu'ran* is read to the patient. The family will encourage the patient to recite, "There is no god but Allah and Mohammed is a messenger of Allah" before dying. The family will assist in washing the body and wrapping it in a white cloth.

Shinto All jewelry is to be removed and the body is washed and dressed in a white kimono.

Taoism The family may wish to have a priest at the bedside at the time of death.

Roman Catholic Anointing of the sick and Holy Communion is encouraged. A rosary service the evening before the funeral is often done.

RELIGIOUS PRAYERS
Jewish Prayer on Behalf of the Sick

May God who blessed those who came before us in history and in life, heal _____ who is ill. May the Holy One, have mercy upon _____; O Lord, reduce the pain and bind the wounds. Give skill to those who help in healing. And speedily restore _____ to perfect health, both spiritual and physical. Amen.

A Prayer for Quiet Confidence
The Very Reverend John Wallace Suter, Fourth Dean of Washington National Cathedral, 1928, *Book of Common Prayer.*

O God of peace, who hast taught us that in returning and rest we shall be saved, in quietness and confidence shall be our strength:

By the might of our Spirit lift us, we pray Thee, to Thy presence, where we may be still and know that Thou art God.

Through Jesus Christ our Lord, Amen.

A Litany for Preserving the Inner Self and the Earth
The Reverend Frederick Quinn, Chair of the Environment Committee of the Commission on Peace of the Diocese of Washington Cathedral.

Lord of the universe, you placed the earth in our trust; help us to preserve it wisely. Help us to cherish ourselves upon this earth in all its mystery. Treasure its fragile beauty and honor its diversity; help us to turn from paths of selfishness and destruction; let all creation reflect God's wonder and all creatures, in their own voices, sing God's praise.

Muslim Prayer of Healing
(The Holy *Qu'ran,* Chapter II: 153-157)

O ye who believe! Seek help with patient persever-ance and prayer; for God is with those who patiently persevere. And say not of those who are slain in the way nay, they are living, though ye perceive it not. Be sure we shall test you with something of fear and hunger, some loss in goods or lives or the fruits of your toil, but give glad tidings to those who patiently persevere. Who say, when afflicted with calamity: "To God we belong, and to Him is our return." They are those on whom descend blessings from God, and mercy, and they are the ones that receive guidance.

A Hindu Prayer for Healing the Body and Spirit

May the Supreme Lord of the Universe nourish the body so that I may have only auspicious words, that I may see only good things, that I may see the divin-ity in all things and everywhere experience the many forms of the One Supreme God: that all people on earth may be blessed.

LEGAL CONSIDERATIONS

Coroner's case Those deaths in which the county coroner must be made aware: deaths such as homicides, suicides, and suspicious or accidental deaths.

Death certificate The legal document that identifies the date, time, and cause(s) of death.

Documentation The date and time of death, along with the health care workers' final activities, should be noted in the client's chart.

Do not resuscitate Because these words may have different meanings for different people, it should be clearly documented what the meaning is for each client. Health care facilities will want to make sure that the wishes of the person and family are being carried out completely and correctly.

Establishing the time of death Absence of response to external stimuli, heart rate, respiration, and pupillary reflexes.

Final disposition Final destination for the body. The hospital or county morgue or funeral home is generally the final disposition of the body.

Life-sustaining procedure Any medical procedure that in the judgment of the physician would only prolong the dying process.

Living will A document that informs the physician that in the event of a terminal illness or injury the person wishes to have life-sustaining procedures stopped or withheld.

Organ donations The law requires all hospitals that receive Medicare dollars to ask for organ donations on death.

Persistent vegetative state A condition of irreversible cessation of all functions of the cerebral cortex that results in a complete chronic and irreversible cessation of all cognitive functions. This condition must be documented by two physicians.

Postmortem/autopsy An examination conducted to determine the exact cause of death.

Power of attorney for health care A legal document in which a person specifies another person to make his or her medical decisions in the event the person cannot.

Pronouncement Certification as to the time of death. In most states, only a physician is responsible for this procedure.

CARE OF THE BODY IMMEDIATELY AFTER DEATH

If the family is *not* present at the time of death:

- Assess to see whether there were any special religious, cultural, or family instructions.
- Review the facility's policies and procedures for preparation.
- Assess to see whether there are any legal limitations in preparing the body.
- Wear gloves when preparing the body.
- The body should be placed flat, arms and legs straight.
- The eyes and mouth should be closed.
- Remove all IV lines, NG tubes, Foley catheters, etc.
- Clean away any excretions/secretions.
- Dress the body in a clean gown, if possible.
- Remove all excess equipment and trash from room.
- Set personal items (dentures/glasses) near the client.
- Pack up all other personal items.
- Document your work in the client's chart and wait for family.

If the family *is* present at the time of death:

- Allow family a few minutes to be with their loved one.
- Ask family if there are any religious or cultural rituals that need to be honored.
- Ask family for a few minutes to prepare the body.
- Allow family to assist with body if they wish.
- Allow family as much time as possible with their loved one.
- Assist the family in packing up the belongings.
- Assist the family with any paperwork.

- Allow family to call nonpresent family members, if needed.
- Support the family in deciding on a funeral home or other arrangements.
- Once the family has gone, prepare the body for removal per the facility's protocol.
- Document your work in the client's chart.

General Guidelines for Autopsies, Burial Versus Cremation, and Organ Donations

	Accepts Autopsies	Burial vs Cremation	May Donate Organs
Agnostic	Yes	Both	Yes
Amish	Yes	Burial	Reluctant
Arab	Discouraged	Burial	Reluctant
Atheist	Yes	Both	Yes
Baha'i	Yes	Burial	Yes
Buddhist	Yes	Cremation	Yes
Cambodian	Yes	Both	Yes
Catholic (Orthodox)	Reluctant	Burial	Reluctant
Catholic (Roman)	Yes	Both	Yes
Chinese	Yes	Both	Yes
Christian	Yes	Both	Yes
Christian Scientist	Reluctant	Both	Reluctant
Eastern Orthodox	Reluctant	Burial	Yes

Filipino	Yes	Both	Yes
Gypsy	Reluctant	Burial	Reluctant
Hindu	Reluctant	Both	Yes
Hispanic	Yes	Both	Yes
Hmong	Yes	Both	Yes
Islamic	Reluctant	Burial	Reluctant
Japanese	Yes	Both	Yes
Jehovah's Witness	Reluctant	Both	Reluctant
Judaism (Hasidim)	Reluctant	Burial	Reluctant
Judaism (Orthodox)	Reluctant	Burial	Reluctant
Judaism (Reform)	Yes	Both	Yes
Korean	Yes	Both	Reluctant
Laotian	Yes	Both	Yes
Mennonite	Yes	Both	Yes

Continued

General Guidelines for Autopsies, Burial Versus Cremation, and Organ Donations—cont'd			
	Accepts Autopsies	Burial vs Cremation	May Donate Organs
Mormon	Yes	Burial	Yes
Native American	Reluctant	Both	Reluctant
Quaker	Yes	Cremation	Yes
Russian Orthodox	Yes	Both	Yes
Seventh Day Adventist	Reluctant	Both	Yes
Shinto	No	Both	No
Sikhism	Reluctant	(Stillborn) Burial (All others) Cremated	Yes
Taoist	Yes	Both	Yes
Thai	Yes	Both	Yes
Vietnamese	Yes	Cremation	Yes

MULTIORGAN PROCUREMENT
Organs and Tissues That Can Be Donated
Organs. Heart, lungs, liver, pancreas, kidneys, intestines.

Bones/Soft Tissues. Humerus, ribs, iliac crest, vertebrae, femur, tibia, fibula, tendons, ligaments, fascia lata.

Other Tissues. Eyes, heart valves, skin, saphenous vein.

Consent Hierarchy
1. Signed donor card
2. Spouse
3. Adult son or daughter
4. Either parent
5. Adult brother or sister
6. Grandparent
7. Legal guardian

Potential Donors
1. Victims of cerebral trauma
2. Trauma victims
3. Some drug overdoses
4. Primary brain tumors
5. Anoxic brain damage
6. Cerebral or subarachnoid bleeds

Special Notes Regarding Procurement
Procuring an organ(s) is a surgical procedure that takes place in the operating room, under sterile techniques.

When applicable, after the procurement, prosthetic replacement and proper suturing are completed to restore the body to its natural appearance.

Donating organs should not interfere with funeral arrangements or with the desire to have an open-casket funeral.

There is no cost to the donating family for the procurement or transplant procedure.

Appendix

English-to-Spanish Translation Guide: Key Medical Questions

The following is a guide to help you complete the history and examination of Spanish-speaking patients. Initial questions presented are general ones used at the beginning of the examination. Questions for pain assessment follow. The remainder of the translations are arranged in order of the body systems. Each system's section contains basic vocabulary, questions used for history taking, and instructions that would facilitate examination. The intent of this guide is to offer an array of questions and phrases from which the examiner can choose as appropriate for assessment.

Hints for Pronunciation of Spanish Words
1. *h* is silent.
2. *j* is pronounced as *h*.
3. *ll* is pronounced as a *y* sound.
4. *r* is pronounced with a trilled sound, and *rr* is trilled even more.
5. *v* is pronounced with a *b* sound.
6. A *y* by itself is pronounced with a long *e* sound.
7. Accent marks over the vowel indicate the syllable that is to be stressed.

Introductory

I am _____.	Soy _____.
What is your name?	¿Cómo se llama usted?
I would like to examine you now.	Quisiera examinarlo(a) ahora.

General

How do you feel?	¿Cómo se siente?
Good	Bien
Bad	Mal
Do you feel better today?	¿Se siente mejor hoy?
Where do you work?	¿Dónde trabaja? (¿Cuál es su profesión o trabajo?) (¿Qué hace usted?)
Are you allergic to anything?	¿Tiene usted algerias?
Medications, foods, insect bites?	¿Medicinas, alimentos, picaduras de insectos?
Do you take any medications?	¿Toma usted algunas medicinas?
Do you have any drug allergies?	¿Es usted alérgico(a) algún médicamento?
Do you have a history of	¿Padece usted enfermedad
heart disease?	del corazón?
diabetes?	del diabetes?
epilepsy?	la epilepsia?
bronchitis?	de bronquitis?
emphysema?	de enfisema?
asthma?	de asma?

From Seidel HM and others: *Mosby's guide to physical examination*, ed 4, St Louis, 1999, Mosby.

Pain

Have you any pain?	¿Tiene dolor?
Where is the pain?	¿Dónde está el dolor?
Do you have any pain here?	¿Tiene usted dolor aqui?
How severe is the pain?	¿Qué tan fuerte es el dolor?
Mild, moderate, sharp, or severe?	¿Ligero, moderado, agudo, severo?
What were you doing when the pain started?	¿Qué haciá usted cuando le comenzó el dolor?
Have you ever had this pain before?	¿Ha tenido este dolor antes?
	(¿Ha sido siempre así?)
Do you have a pain in your side?	¿Tiene usted dolor en el costado?
Is it worse now?	¿Está peor ahora?
Does it still pain you?	¿Le duele todavía?
Did you feel much pain at the time?	¿Sintió mucho dolor entonces?
Show me where.	Muéstreme dónde.
Does it hurt when I press here?	¿Le duele cuando aprieto aquí?

Head

Vocabulary

Head	La cabeza
Face	La cara

History

How does your head feel?	¿Cómo siente la cabeza?
Have you any pain in the head?	¿Le duele la cabeza?
Do you have headaches?	¿Tiene usted dolores de cabeza?

Do you have migranes? | ¿Tiene usted migrañas?
What causes the headaches? | ¿Qué le causa los dolores de cabeza?

Examination
Lift up your head. | Levante la cabeza.

Eyes
Vocabulary
Eye | El ojo

History
Have you had pain in your eyes? | ¿Ha tenido dolor en los ojos?
Do you wear glasses? | ¿Usa usted anteojos/ gafas/lentes/ espejuelos?

Do you wear contact lenses? | ¿Usa usted lentes de contacto?
Can you see clearly? Better at a distance? | ¿Puede ver claramente? ¿Mejor a cierta distancia?

Do you sometimes see things double? | ¿Ve las cosas doble algunas veces?
Do you see things through a mist? | ¿Ve las cosas nubladas?
Were you exposed to anything that could have injured your eye? | ¿Fue expuesto a cualquier cosa que pudiera haberle dañado el ojo?
Do your eyes water much? | ¿Le lagrimean mucho los ojos?

Examination
Look up. | Mire para arriba.
Look down. | Mire para abajo.

Look toward your nose.	Mírese la nariz.
Look at me.	Míreme.
Tell me what number it is.	Digame qué número es éste.
Tell me what letter it is.	Digame qué letra es ésta.

Ears/Nose/Throat
Vocabulary

Ears	Los oídos
Eardrum	El tímpano
Laryngitis	La laringitis
Lip	El labio
Mouth	La boca
Nose	La naríz
Tongue	La lengua

History

Do you have any hearing problems?	¿Tiene usted problemas de oir?
Do you use a hearing aid?	¿Usa usted un audífono?
Do you have ringing in the ears?	¿Le zumban los oídos?
Do you have allergies?	¿Tiene alergias?
Do you use dentures?	¿Usa usted dentadura postiza?
Do you have any loose teeth, removable bridges, or any prosthesis?	¿Tiene dientes flojos, dientes postizos, o cualquier prostesis?
Do you have a cold?	¿Tiene usted un resfriado/resfrío?
Do you have sore throats frequently?	¿Le duele la garganta con frecuencia?
Have you ever had a strep throat?	¿Ha tenido alguna vez (infección de la garganta)?

Examination

Open your mouth.	Abra la boca.
I want to take a throat culture.	Quiero hacer un cultivo de la garganta.
This will not hurt.	Esto no le va a doler.

Cardiovascular

Vocabulary

Heart	El corazón
Heart attack	El ataque al corazón
Heart disease	La enfermedad del corazón
Heart murmur	El soplo del corazón
High blood pressure	Alta presión

History

Have you ever had any chest pain?	¿Ha tenido alguna vez dolor de pecho?
Where?	¿Dónde?
Do you notice any irregularity of heart beat or any palpitations?	¿Nota cualquier latido o palpitación irregular?
Do you get short of breath?	¿Tiene usted problemas con la respiracion?
When?	¿Cuándo?
Do you take medicine for your heart?	¿Toma medicina para el corazón?
How often?	¿ Con qué frecuencia?
Do you know if you have high blood pressure?	¿Sabe usted si tiene la presión alta?
Is there a history of hypertension in your family?	¿En su familia se encuentron varias personas con alta presión?

Are any of your limbs swollen?	¿Están hinchados algunos de sus miembros?
Hands, feet, legs?	¿Manos, pies, piernas?
How long have they been swollen like this?	¿Desde cuándo están hinchados así? (¿Qué tanto tiempo tiene usted con esta inchason?)

Examination

Let me feel your pulse.	Déjeme tomarle el pulso.
I am going to take your blood pressure now.	Le voy a tomar la presión ahora.

Respiratory

Vocabulary

Chest	El pecho
Lungs	Los pulmones

History

Do you smoke? How many packs a day?	¿Fuma usted? ¿Cuántos paquetes al día?
Have you any difficulty in breathing?	¿Tiene dificultad al respirar?
How long have you been coughing?	¿Desde cuándo tiene tos?
Do you cough up phlegm?	¿Al toser, escupe usted flema(s)?
What is the color of your expectorations?	¿Cuándo usted escupe, qué color es?
Do you cough up blood?	¿Al toser, arroja usted sangre?
Do you wheeze?	¿Le silba a usted el pecho?

Examination

Take a deep breath.	Respìre profundo.
Breathe normally.	Respìre normalmente.
Cough.	Tosa.
Cough again.	Tosa otra vez.

Gastrointestinal

Vocabulary

Abdomen	El abdomen
Intestines/bowels	Los intestinos/las entrañas
Liver	El hígado
Nausea	Náusea
Gastric ulcer	La úlcera gástrica
Stomach	El estomago, la panza, la barriga
Stomachache	El dolor de estómago

History

What foods disagree with you?	¿Qué alimentos le caen mal?
Do you get heartburn?	¿Suele tener ardor en el pecho?
Do you have indigestion often?	¿Tiene indigestión con frecuencia?
Are you going to vomit?	¿Va a vomitar-(arrojar)?
Do you have blood in your vomit?	¿Tiene usted vómitos con sangre?
Do you have abdominal pain?	¿Tiene dolor en el abdomen?
How are your stools?	¿Cómo son sus defecaciones?
Are they regular?	¿Son regulares?
Have you noticed their color?	¿Se ha fijado en el color?
Are you constipated?	¿Está estreñido?
Do you have diarrhea?	¿Tiene diarrea?

Genitourinary
Vocabulary

Genitals	Los genitales
Kidney	El riñón
Penis	El pene, el miembro
Urine	La orina

History

Have you any difficulty passing water?	¿Tiene dificultad en orinar?
Do you pass water involuntarily?	¿Orina sin querer?
Do you have a urethral discharge?	¿Tiene descho de la uretra?
Do you have burning with urination?	¿Tiene ardor al orinar?

Musculoskeletal
Vocabulary

Ankle	El tobillo
Arm	El brazo
Back	La espalda
Bones	Los huesos
Elbow	El codo
Finger	El dedo
Foot	El pie
Fracture	La fractura
Hand	La mano
Hip	La cadera
Knee	La rodilla
Leg	La pierna
Muscles	Los músculos
Rib	La costilla
Shoulder	El hombro
Thigh	El muslo

History

Did you fall and how did you fall?	¿Se cayó, y cómo se cayó?
How did this happen? How long ago?	¿Cómo sucedío esto? ¿Cuanto tiempo hace?

Examination

Raise your arm.	Levante el brazo.
Raise it more.	Más alto.
Now the other.	Ahora el otro.
Stand up and walk.	Parese y camine.
Straighten your leg.	Enderece la pierna.
Bend your knee.	Doble la rodilla.
Push	Empuje
Pull	Jale
Up	Arriba
Down	Abajo
In/out	Adentro/afuera
Rest	Descanse
Kneel	Arrodíllese

Neurologic

Vocabulary

Brain	El cerebro
Dizziness	El vértigo, el mareo
Epilepsy	La epilepsia
Fainting spell	El desmayo
Unconscious	La insensibilidad (inconsiente)

History

Have you ever had a head injury?	¿Ha tenido alguna vez daño a la cabeza?
Do you have convulsions?	¿Tiene convulsiones?
Do you have tingling sensations?	¿Tiene hormigueos?
Do you have numbness in your hands, arms, or feet?	¿Siente entumecidos las manos, los brazos, o los pies?
Have you ever lost consciousness?	¿Perdió alguna vez el sentido? (inconsiente)
For how long?	¿Por cuánto tiempo?
How often does this happen?	¿Con qué frecuencia ocurre esto?

Examination

Squeeze my hand.	Apriete mi mano.
Can you not do it better than that?	¿No puede hacerlo más fuerte?
Turn on your left/right side.	Voltéese al lado izquierdo/al lado derechos.
Roll over and sit up over the edge of the bed.	Voltéese y siéntese sobre el borde del la cama.
Stand up slowly. Put your weight only on your right/left foot.	Párese despacio. Ponga peso sólo en la pierna derecha/izquierda.
Take a step to the side.	Dé un paso al lado.
Turn to your left/right.	Doble a la izquierda/ derecha.
Is this hot or cold?	¿Está frío o caliente esto?
Am I sticking you with the point or the head of the pin?	¿Le estoy pinchando con la cabeza del alfiler?

Endocrine/Reproductive
Vocabulary

Uterus	El útero, la matríz
Vagina	La vagina

History

Have you had any problems with your thyroid?	¿Ha tenido alguna vez problemas con tiroides?
Have you noticed any significant weight gain or loss?	¿Ha notado pérdida o aumento de peso?
What is your usual weight?	¿Cuál es su peso usual?
How is your appetite?	¿Qué tal su apetito?

Women:

How old were you when your periods started?	¿Cuántos años tenía cuando tuvo la primera regla?
How many days between periods?	¿Cuántos días entre las reglas?
When was your last menstrual period?	¿Cuándo fue su última regla?
Have you ever been pregnant?	¿Ha estado embarazada?
How many children do you have?	¿Cuántos hijos tiene?
When was your last Pap smear?	¿Cuándo fue su última prueba de Papanicolado?
Would you like information on birth control methods?	¿Quiere usted información sobre los métodos del control de la natalidad?
Do you have a vaginal discharge?	¿Tiene descho vaginales?

✳ Index

Page numbers followed by f
indicate figures; t, tables.

LOOK-ALIKE AND SOUND-ALIKE MEDICATIONS

A Common Cause for Medication Errors

Accupril	Accutane
Accupril	Monopril
acetohexamide	acetazolamide
Allegra	Viagra
Alora	Aldara
alprazolam	lorazepam
Ansaid	Asacol
Asacol	Os-Cal
asparaginase	pegaspargase
Bumex	Buprenex
Bumex	Permax
Calan	Colace
Cardene	Cardizem
carvedilol	captopril
carvedilol	carteolol
cefazolin	cefprozil
Cefol	Cefzil
Cefotan	Ceftin
codeine	Cardene
codeine	iodine
codeine	Lodine
cyclobenzaprine	cyproheptadine
cyclophosphamide	cyclosporine
Cytosar-U	Cytovene
Cytotec	Cytoxan
Darvon	Diovan
Demerol	Desyrel
Denavir	indinavir
diazepam	lorazepam
Diovan	Zyban
doxorubicin	daunorubicin